Studies in the government
and control of education since 1860

Reprinted from the

HISTORY OF
EDUCATION SOCIETY'S

Studies in the government and control of education since 1860

Published by

METHUEN & CO LTD

11 New Fetter Lane EC4

First published 1970
by Methuen & Co Ltd
11 New Fetter Lane, London EC4
© 1970 by History of Education
Society
Set in Press Roman by
Santype (Coldtype) Ltd
Salisbury, Wilts.
Printed in Great Britain by
Redwood Press,
Trowbridge, Wilts.
SBN 416 15380 1

Distributed in the U.S.A.
by Barnes & Noble Inc.

Contents

Preface

The five papers in this collection, bearing on 'The Government and Control of Education' in the nineteenth and twentieth centuries, were delivered at a conference of the History of Education Society on 21–22 December 1968. This marked the end of the first year's work of the Society which was formed with the aim of broadening studies in the history of education and stimulating interest in all aspects of the subject. As the papers given broke new ground, even in the well-worked field of nineteenth-century educational developments, there was a strong demand for publication. With a growing interest in the subject generally, and not only in departments and colleges of education, it has been found possible to publish in book form. We hope that this will be the first of a number of volumes sponsored by the Society.

As an introduction to the conference Mr Stuart Maclure, then editor of *Education* but editor-elect of *The Times Educational Supplement*, spoke on 'The Control of Education' in a contemporary context but with many historical references. Various cherished assumptions were then challenged by Mr Norman Morris – of the Department of Education of the University of Manchester, where much higher degree work centres on the government and administration of education – in a paper on 'State Intervention and *Laissez-Faire* in the 1860s'. There followed concentration on a more limited, but neglected, field, the Technical Instruction Committees of the 1890s in a paper by Dr P. H. J. H. Gosden of the Department of Education, University of Leeds.

It has been a special concern of the Society to pay attention to developments in Wales and Scotland, so frequently omitted from the teaching programmes of English institutions, and the last two papers, based on research into the records of the Welsh and Scottish Education Departments respectively, should help to remedy this deficiency. A comprehensive survey of the evolution of the Welsh system of secondary and higher education after the Aberdare Report of 1881 (which owing to exigencies of space has been abridged in the present volume) was given by Dr Leslie Wynne Evans of the Department of Education, Cardiff University College; and Mr John Stocks, of the University of Dundee, gave an illuminating account of a development almost unknown outside Scotland, but of interest to all students of administration, in a paper on the *ad hoc* authorities which were in being from 1919 to 1930.

The Society is very grateful to Mrs Joan Simon for helping to prepare the papers for publication and to Mr D. S. Hempsall for compiling the index. Mr Malcolm Seaborne saw the book through the press on the Society's behalf. Enquiries about membership of the History of Education Society, which is open to all engaged in teaching or studying the subject, should be addressed to the Secretary, Mr Ian Taylor, at St John's College, York, YO3 7EX.

David C. A. Bradshaw

Sheffield City College of Education

Chairman, History of Education Society

STUART MACLURE

The control of education

It seems to me an open question whether English education is controlled at all. I wrote somewhere recently that there is a sense in which, today, education is out of control. In many respects its development is more plausibly explained in terms of challenge and response, springing from fundamental attitudes which are themselves changing in the face of a social and technological revolution, than as the result of the explicit pursuit of particular policies by those who pull the levers of power. Anyway I am always a bit suspicious of the levers of power. We know that many of those which educational policy makers seek to pull don't work, or produce results quite different from those expected.

Control seems altogether too precise a term. It has distinct scientific overtones. Research workers set up controlled experiments like the educational psychologist whose wife gave birth to twins. He had one baptised and kept the other as a control.

In yet another sense, control somehow suggests something mechanical. There are control 'systems' and control engineers. Inevitably it conjures up a picture of something more systematic, more subject to formal direction, than what we know of education. Perhaps this is an error which an historical approach is liable to encourage. It is uncommonly easy to attribute motive and clear-cut aims where they never existed and to be carried along by an evolutionary myth which turns history into a self-conscious succession of ghosts and embryos. The metaphors can all too easily take over. Control, for example, seems to imply a controller or controllers; some masterful figure somewhere, ensconced, it may be, appropriately enough, in a control tower, directing the affairs of education like the man at London airport who talks down the fog-bound 707s; or the asthmatic character called 'control' at the end of the crackling loudspeaker who barks instructions to taxi-drivers. As we all know, the government and control of

1

education in this country doesn't happen to be like that at all. It is a great deal more complicated and a great deal less systematic.

I think some such warning as this needs to be sounded at the outset because of what I take to be the essential paradox of English education: that the more coherent our education system has become, the more complex and diffuse the controls have become. In other words, the more education has come to be organized into an articulated whole, the looser, more varied and more widely distributed have been the controls which determine what kind of education the system dispenses.

The pattern of control as I visualize it is a network like the grid on an ordnance survey map. On one axis are the formal, legal and administrative controls exercised under statute by government, local authorities, the churches, and indirectly by other bodies such as the University Grants Committee. If you like, these are the vertical lines on the grid — the framework of power and authority through which socio-political decisions are mediated on matters of finance and administration.

The horizontal lines in this network represent the other controls which stem from professional, academic, social and commercial sources — for example, the controls on the content of education exercised by the examining bodies, the educational publishers, the teachers and indirectly by parents and employers outside the school system.

At certain key points the grid lines intermesh — the financial and administrative controls cut across the professional and academic. For example teacher supply determines what teaching methods are possible and what can be taught. So do buildings.

Sometimes this interaction brings about change which in time comes to be formalized — like the process by which governing bodies have in practice lost control of curriculum (which in many cases is still technically theirs) to the teachers, who themselves are in varying degree and at different times subject to rigorous pressures of 11-plus selection, examining bodies, university admissions officers and so on.

Sometimes it is a question of seeking new administrative techniques to temper the cold force of finance — as when members of the University Grants Committee, under pressure to rationalize, find themselves intervening in the curriculum through their subject committees.

Perhaps this last example illustrates the complexity of analysing some aspects of the control of education. The fact that in the case of the universities much of the pressure has taken place over anchovy toast upstairs at the Athenaeum, instead of by circulars or directives, doesn't remove it from the network of control. Sometimes, as with the Schools

Council, an elaborate new device is created which is itself a microcosmic version of the larger network.

If I can carry the analogy or metaphor one stage further — the system depends on the net being kept in tension: hence the powerful pressure groups pulling away at the corners of the net; and the elaborate processes of consultation by which each source of power shares it, to some extent at least, with rival power groups. Hence the vigorous life of the local authority associations, the teachers unions, the unions, the churches (admittedly mainly when they are seeking more money for denominational schools, or scenting a change in the law about religious education)[1].

In essence, all these power groups tend to be centralizing forces. Even the local authority bodies which exist to preserve the independence of local authorities from the growing power of central direction, end up as instruments of uniformity. The more they can persuade the central government to accept them as spokesmen for, and guardians of, the local interest, the more they have to whip their members into line: so power and control is absorbed to the centre, yet, at the centre, it is distributed between government and the central organizations of local government. (In parenthesis: I am highly sceptical of the suggestion that larger units of local government will lead to a devolution of control: stronger local government units will cause the central government to be even more firm in reserving control to the centre.) The teachers' unions have a similar paradoxical role to play. All this makes it harder than ever for the consumers to organize peripheral pressure into a national force — which the Confederation for the Advancement of State Education can never effectively be.

Looked at historically, it seems to me the motif is plain. Initially there is no distinction between the vertical and the horizontal lines on the grid — the financial and administrative, and the curricular and the professional are intertwined in a single and formidable thick black line. This unitary control is most clearly expressed in the period of 'payment by results'. By the end of the century the single strand has been split up and not only is the administrative and financial framework becoming more diversified but the professional interest is becoming organized and effective. The horizontal lines appear, and the basis of the present pattern is laid. Lastly I shall suggest that there are reasons to suppose that the combined effect of curriculum reform and educational technology will be to bring about a new combination of the vertical and the horizontal lines, and to demand a new compromise between financial and curriculum control.

Now let us consider the way in which this network came about. In simpler times, control and ownership went together. Motives for starting schools varied: for the churches ownership expressed the prescriptive right to provide education as the by-product of some other, more evangelical aim. Everyone is familiar with some of the more bizarre consequences of this kind of control by ownership. The Rev. Jabez Bunting, pope of early nineteenth-century Methodism, intervened in wrath in the Sunday school at his Sheffield church to stop writing from being taught, because writing was a secular art inappropriate to the Sabbath, unlike reading which, in its way, was a spiritual grace. Control didn't stop at what happened in school. Church schools could demand church attendance on Sundays, even from those who might normally go with their parents to a nonconformist chapel.

In the case of the old endowed schools the rudiment of control was a trust deed which, as interpreted by Lord Eldon and others in the Court of Chancery, ensured that the dead hand of a founder continued to govern the curriculum. Here matters could only be modified by time and the pressure of such reports as those of the Clarendon and Taunton Commissions and their successor bodies. In the same way it took legislation to unlock the Oxford and Cambridge colleges from the dead grasp of misguided benefactors and the conditions they had imposed: the mid-century Royal Commissions record numerous examples of scholarships and fellowships reserved to founders' kin and other restrictions from beyond the grave.

Even in these mid-nineteenth-century times, control can be recognized in indirect as well as direct form. Behind the control which stemmed from ownership there was the pressure exerted by the power of the purse. Industrialists, no less than theologians, were apt to object to what a school failed to do, or worse, to what it tried to do. The Rev. Henry Moseley, M.A., F.R.S., H.M. Inspector of Schools, wrote many reports which contain sharp fragments of social history. In 1846 he reported on schools in South Staffordshire where earnings were high, yet the social tone was, in his view, regrettably low.

> The miners of Bilston are 5,000 in number and it is computed that £50,000 are spent by them annually in the purchase of ale·. . . In no schools that I have visited has it been found necessary to fix the fees of admission lower . . . An opulent proprietor had, at the period of my last visit to the schools in his district, withdrawn his subscription of £1 because writing had, against his judgment, been added to the subjects of instruction.

He went on to tell how there was one ray of hope. The Savings Bank had begun to attract depositors. A gentleman had told Mr Moseley of his success in encouraging a workman to start to save. 'At the end of five years he drew out the fund he had accumulated, amounting, I think, to £13, bought a piece of land, and has built a house on it.' This was money which — as Mr Moseley's informant pointed out — 'would have been spent on feasting or clubs or contributions to the trade union'. He concludes: 'that man's eyes are now open — his social position is raised — he sees and feels as we do, and will influence others to follow his example'[2].

By this time — the time Mr Moseley was on his travels — the first elements of system and control had been introduced in the shape of grants from the Committee of Council and the critical decision to set up an inspectorate. The issue of public control is thus from the first, as might be expected, linked with finance. Even so, the Minute of 1840 which gave the inspectors their charge could hardly have been more explicit in rejecting the idea of direction: 'It is of the utmost consequence that you should bear in mind that this inspection is not intended as a means of exercising control but of affording assistance'[3].

But government grants and the Inspectorate — though introduced to encourage and guide voluntary effort — carried their own logic. The social and intellectual gulf between the H.M.I.s and the teachers ensured that any relationship would be an unequal one. Anyway, encouragement was expensive and by the 1860s it was hardly surprising that a Revised Code should be prepared which offered both closer control over expenditure and closer control over what was taught. An incomparable phrase-maker like Robert Lowe had little difficulty in making this sound like a way of getting better value for money. Incidentally in the 1850s there was a period when public education expenditure was rising even faster than it has been rising since the end of the Second World War, and without a comparable inflation.

Of course the Revised Code and payment by results introduced a much more rigid form of control discussed elsewhere by Mr Norman Morris. But pernicious as the consequences of the code may have been, the control through grant and inspection which existed beforehand was held by many to have encouraged teaching programmes which showed more ambition than realism. There may well have been a good deal to react against. I came across a comment in a report prepared for the London School Board in 1900 which referred to remarkable developments in infants' education before the Revised Code. According to the author, Mr Thomas Alfred Spalding: 'not only were reading writing and arithmetic taught' — this was for the 3 to 6s — 'but sometimes geography, and history, *in a manner well calculated to develop premature stupidity* '[4] .

There were two essential requirements for any serious attempt to get away from this unified control. The first was some local administration; the second was a better educated teaching profession with a stronger professional status. These two developments were attended by a third: the emergence of a new profession of educational administrator.

There is no shortage of evidence to show that elementary school teachers were held in low esteem. You will remember the Newcastle Commission's judgement. The Commission had received complaints that 'the trained teachers are conceited and dissatisfied'. They commented: 'The first we do not believe to be true of the class, the second we admit to a certain degree, and account for it by remarking, amongst other causes, that their emoluments, though not too low, rise too soon to their highest level'.

The Revised Code was deliberately anti-teacher and hence opposed to any independent initiative on curriculum in elementary education. Grants were to be paid direct to managers with whom the Education Department would communicate. Robert Lowe again:

> The great danger is that the grant for education may become a grant to maintain the so-called vested interest of those engaged in education. If parliament does not set a limit to this evil, such a state of things will arise that the conduct of the educational system will pass out of the hands of the Privy Council and of the House of Commons into the hands of the persons working that educational system, and then no demand they choose to make on the public purse would any Ministry dare to refuse.

Here is the key to the control of education up to the 1890s, grasped with typically tactless brutality by Lowe. Until this rigid control began to break up there could only be limited progress; yet what progress there was — particularly in quantity — hastened to break it up.

The school boards after 1870 helped to chip away at the codes and the system. Being democratic bodies, they represented a new source of political power and because they could raise a rate they could afford to go beyond the limitations of the code. They also provided a new political focus for teachers, as the growth of the National Union of Elementary Teachers indicated, and as the frequent complaints of the teachers' undue influence in school board matters began to confirm.

I have recently been reading my way into the affairs of the London

School Board and certainly the first superficial impression to be derived from the official papers and from the memoirs of people like Beatrice Webb is that it was the members who made the running in London, and that, quite deliberately, the officers were kept in a subordinate position. There were at the outset people like T. H. Huxley to chair the curriculum committee. Each School Board member had local responsibilities as a leading member of a local school committee as well as his duties at Spring Gardens. The early concern of members in the social questions of education – their immediate grasp of matters spelled out painfully word by word in the Newsom Report –reflected the wise instincts of the interested amateur.

In London, at least, the contrast with the Technical Education Board could hardly have been greater. Sidney Webb, the first chairman, aimed high from the start and any account of the control of technical education would have to weigh up the work of the Board's secretary, William Garnett.

It was the 1902 Act, the county and county borough councils and the Part III authorities which gave chief education officers a new importance and wider responsibilities. Gradually more and more of them were professional teachers turned to administration, instead of clerks who had become drawn into educational work.

This progression has yet to be investigated. My guess is that the increasing self-consciousness of the C.E.O.s has been a factor in promoting the autonomy of the professionals in matters of curriculum. The C.E.O. was the professional as well as the administrative adviser to the local authority. He was the natural enemy of H.M.I. and the natural defender of the schools against Ministry of Education control. His own professional interest inclined him to discourage his committee members from taking too close an interest in curriculum and content. As an ex-teacher, he tended to contribute to the newly orthodox view of professional status for teachers. A succession of great C.E.O.s like Spurley Hey, James Graham, Percival Sharp and Brockington, fought and won the battle for recognition with the Ministry of Education. Some were super-headmasters. Some, like Sharp – one of the arche-types – were very tough indeed. Others, like Henry Morris of a slightly later period, were deeply committed to liberal views about education. All helped to diversify the control of education, and, directly or indirectly, to build up the horizontal lines on my grid.

The quality and progressiveness of the local authorities might differ, as might the attitude of the central department at particular times and on particular matters, but in terms of control and the power structure a norm was early established which has continued till very recently, that on the whole, in the sharing of control between the centre and the periphery, the centre has had the function of regulation and restriction, while at the periphery there has been pressure to do more and to go faster. Not everywhere, nor all the time; but this is the conventional relationship. Here again personalities enter in, particularly in the second half of the nineteenth century. It was this tension, temporarily released by men like A. H. Dyke Acland in the nineties and accentuated by the activities of the Science and Art Department, and the distribution of the 'whisky money', that exploded the administrative shell of the 1870 Act, and made it impossible to confine the system within the contemporary definition of elementary education. And it is arguable that it was this tension which finally shattered the unity of the financial and the curricular control and released the creative energies of the teaching profession.

The elementary schools were the first to be organized into a system. It is inevitable that control should be discussed in terms of the elementary school system. But after 1902, when local education authorities succeeded school boards and the secondary schools were linked to the system, new types of control − through the secondary school examinations − were carried over into the public system and the network of authority became steadily more complicated. The early county grammar schools were closely regulated by the Board of Education, and the curriculum in all elementary schools remained in the charge of the managers. The teachers' independence was still a very long way off. But change was beginning to take place, as usual, from the infant school upwards. May I refer again to the report prepared for the London School Board in 1900, to which Miss Phillips, the superintendent of method, contributed a chapter on infant schools? There is something familiar about all this: 'Now', wrote Miss Phillips,

we are beginning to understand that ideas precede language and language precedes its expression in written or printed characters. In our best infants' schools the old drudgery of alphabet learning and dreary sing-song spelling of words are disappearing and each teacher makes for herself some bright, interesting combination of 'Look and Say' and 'Phonic method' [5].

The point about this, I think, is that it did not arise from a monolithic system of control. It derived from a more informed understanding; and the method of propagation was as much through the slow and painful process of teacher education as anything. It is very noticeable that the development of more diversified methods of control coincided with more and better methods of teacher training. By the same token, the Revised Code coincided with a period when the state withdrew some of its support for teacher training.

So the network grew. The teachers gained the *de facto* control of the curriculum which, with all its limitations, they now have, sharing it with the examining bodies – the School Certificate dates from 1917 – with the universities and with the educational publishers. Among the limitations, of course, for much of the time was the relatively static professional view of the curriculum and a widespread acceptance of conventions about what 'subjects' comprised and what content was traditionally appropriate. There can be little doubt that the strength of this conventional wisdom helped to make the teacher control acceptable. People are always more willing to entrust others with freedom if they are confident it won't be used.

So long as an elementary system existed alongside the secondary, vestiges of the old form of curricular control continued. The gradual increase in the number of free places in secondary schools served to highlight this, in that it focused attention on curriculum differences between the upper parts of the elementary system and the secondary schools. Moreover the need to provide a bridge between the elementary and secondary systems – a bridge which took the form of a competition at 10-plus – was by itself a severe constraint on the curriculum of the elementary school, helping to encourage the process of streaming which accompanied promotion by age-groups. Here again was another instance of the governmental, administrative controls and the curricular, professional controls interlinking. For many years before 1944 – and beyond – the selection procedures represented in the minds of most teachers and administrators alike, not restrictive control but the attempt to promote wider opportunity and social justice. To that extent there was no conflict between the agents of administrative and professional control.

The combination of events and the new insights which have caused this to change are matters of recent history. Looked at in longer terms, the move towards secondary education for all, and its logical extension in the direction of comprehensive education, fit into the larger pattern as part of the progressive strengthening of the professional control of the curriculum.

What is the present position? The public control of education, exercised by the D.E.S. and by the local education authorities is operated through the Rate Support Grant, through the supply and training of teachers, the capital programme, the building regulations, and through all the mandatory and discretional duties of the Department and the local authorities under the 1944 Act.

But the whole movement towards curriculum reform introduces a new element — the organized desire for change which somehow has to be orchestrated, yet must not infringe the freedom of the teacher.

The example of large scale curriculum reform has come from America where the diversity of administrative control is prodigious — 51 states and 22,000 school boards — but each school board may control curriculum closely, and overall is a mighty umbrella of theoretical pedagogy which exercises a powerful unifying influence.

What happened here when Sir David Eccles first tried to take a hand in curricular reforms is an object lesson in one aspect of the control of English education. He set up the Curriculum Study Group in 1962 within the Ministry of Education. The model was the architectural development group in which architects, H.M.I.s and administrators combined to thrash out new ideas on school building. But the Curriculum Study Group was still-born. A row with the teachers and the local authorities on pay focused suspicion on this excursion into what was held to be, for the Ministry, forbidden territory. It was not till eighteen months later that Sir Edward Boyle could take the idea further by adopting a complicated constitution of checks and balances between the educational interests worked out by Mr Derek Morrell (since translated to the Home Office) whose creative administration continued when he became one of the first joint secretaries of the Schools Council. The Council is now financed in part directly by the Department, in larger part by the L.E.A.s who control financial policy, while the teachers' unions have a majority on the education policy committees. It sounds like a recipe to confirm Robert Lowe's worst fears.

Following in the steps of Nuffield, the Schools Council has embarked on curriculum projects which are now beginning to come to fruition, and which will bring to the schools educational materials which have been tested and modified in the light of experience. In some cases examinations will change as a consequence. Two of the existing controls are thus being adapted to new circumstances. In-service training, the logical corollary to curriculum reform, modifies the teachers themselves.

But the vertical and the horizontal controls remain separate. Historically, in our particular environment, I have no doubt whatever that this has been a source of strength and has released creative forces.

So has the diversification of the legal and administrative control. The process is still going on. Paradoxically again, a consequence of bringing the universities within some kind of structure or system – the effect of Robbins – has been an increase in the autonomy of the colleges of education and the colleges of further education in the maintained section.

In conclusion, I think the signs are that new control mechanisms will be needed in the not too distant future. Curriculum reform and educational technology will sooner or later present the need for decisions on the grand scale which combine the administrative and financial with the curricular and professional controls. An obvious example is an educational television system. The decision to equip a network of schools and set up a system is akin to a decision to start a school. But the decision on what to teach by ETV affects all the schools and all the teachers. So far it is handled by elaborate teacher committees. But this is only the beginning of the road.

The next stage may well come as the educational technologists seek to apply a systems approach to learning and teaching generally. This points to large investment in the preparation of materials – 'teacher-proof packages' – which can only be justified by the large-scale use of materials which, having been tested and validated, can be proved to work. Before long this will demand decisions on curriculum methods, administration and finance, extending far beyond the boundaries of the largest local authority school system. Sooner or later, this is where the really important educational decisions may lie, and at this stage I can hear the cry going up that education is too important to leave to the teachers or even to stage armies of representative teachers. When it does, the government and control of education will enter a new and perhaps hazardous phase.

Notes

[1] A text book case study of Roman Catholic techniques in the education lobby relates to the 1959 Education Act, one of those which reduced the contribution voluntary school authorities had to make to the capital cost of an 'aided school'; see Tudor David, *Church and School*, pp.7–8, Councils and Education Press Ltd., 1961.

[2] Quoted in Stuart Maclure, *Educational Documents England and Wales, 1816–1967*, p. 57, Chapman and Hall, 1968.

[3] Ibid., pp. 48–49.
[4] T. A. Spalding, *The Work of the London School Board*, P. S. King, 1900.
[5] Ibid.

NORMAN MORRIS

State paternalism and
laissez-faire in the 1860s

Teachers of history tend, of necessity, to make certain assumptions and to attach certain labels or descriptions to people and events. What I want to do here is to consider two generalizations that are frequently made about the history of education in the nineteenth century.

In the first place, we agree that the nineteenth century saw successive acts of governmental intervention which culminated in state assumption of collective responsibility for education. This represented a move from individualism to collectivism. But we also believe that the ethos of the nineteenth century was predominantly individualistic and anti-collectivist. Since there is a contradiction here we go on to conclude that acts of state intervention in education must have been made reluctantly, by people who were gradually pushed along that road against their better judgement.

The second generalization is a related one. Since the nineteenth century saw the emergence of conscious, and even aggressive, *laissez-faire* theory in the economic sphere, it is assumed that this theory must be woven into our interpretation of educational development. Thus, Robert Lowe was a free-trader; therefore, payment by results, the product of a free-trade mind, must reflect a free-trade philosophy.

From these generalizations there derives the following interpretation: mid-nineteenth-century politicians were predominantly *laissez-faire* in outlook but were forced by circumstances, and probably against their will, into acceptance of collective action in the educational field.

Sketching this approach in another way, we often say that eighteenth-century paternalism, which survived into the early nineteenth century, gave way to *laissez-faire* in the expansionist mid-century period; and *laissez-faire* was itself superseded by collectivism towards the end of the century. It might be a mistake, however, to suppose that this progression − even if it took place − happened evenly over all aspects of life. What I want to suggest is that to read educational

13

history against a picture of a generalized progression of this sort may obscure more than it explains.

If any government was ever influenced by free-trade principles, and likely to carry them over into the field of education, it was indeed the government in which Robert Lowe was Minister of Education. It was under Lowe's ministry that the Kay-Shuttleworth system was abandoned and payment by results initiated. This, it is said, inaugurated the sad years during which the state attempted to obtain efficiency in education by purchase. Lowe was a celebrated free-trader and therefore his system represented the triumph of a *laissez-faire* attitude towards state intervention in education.

Now I find this line of thought difficult to follow. It overlooks the fact that the prime object of the Kay-Shuttleworth system itself had been to buy efficiency, by offering money to managers to stimulate school building, by using the purse to nudge managers into buying materials and equipment, by paying teachers to become better qualified, and so on. The whole purpose of making grants-in-aid which foster development is to promote efficiency by the use of money. The argument in 1861 was not whether public money should be used for the first time to promote efficiency, but what was the most effective and least objectionable way in which to continue conducting the purchase of efficiency.

The Kay-Shuttleworth system paid out money for specified purposes but its weakness had been that it lacked sanction. Conditions of grant had no statutory basis and were only enforceable under normal civil contract law. Even this would probably not be used against a defaulter since managers were voluntary workers and, if proceeded against, had only to walk out in order to defeat the whole grant-aid exercise. The grant was simply a carrot for willing horses; in effect, the state offered to double whatever was put in locally, but if the managers defaulted the money was, for practical purposes, irrecoverable. Inspectors were sent round to see if schools were complying with conditions of grant but they were not enforcement officers since there was no law to enforce; all they could do was suggest and report. Now it is not necessary to be a free marketeer, or a butcher of educational expenditure, to find this sort of situation unsatisfactory.

Historians of education have slipped too easily into identifying a system which tried to reward efficiency with a free-market system. It is true that under payment by results the efficiency of teachers was tested by outsiders and the amount of profit earned was geared to the verdict of the testers. But this is far removed from a free-market system.

Payment was made from public money, under conditions closely defined by the state. The fact that the state was cost-conscious does not alter the fact that this was still a publicly provided and publicly controlled service. Economic deployment of resources, and the desire to get value for money expended, are not the hallmarks of free traders. These things are important to anyone — a communist government or a private venture businessman — who is spending money. There is also a tendency to describe the Lowe system as *competitive*. This too can be misleading. The Revised Code re-introduced free bargaining between employer and employed; there may, therefore, have been an element of competition between employers to purchase the services of the best teachers, or between teachers to obtain posts by under-selling their services, and there may have been competition between teachers to achieve results which would enhance their own market value. But the payments themselves were not earned competitively. The state did not establish a fixed fund and set the schools to compete against one another, to see which could get most out of it. Payment on results was a productivity award.

To call the system competitive is to tar it with the *laissez-faire*, market economy brush. Call it a system of organized productivity awards and it becomes respectable, even to collectivists and socialists. In fact, the government in 1862 deliberately rejected any suggestion of state withdrawal from education and any reversion to a free market in schools. It was firmly opposed to relaxation of state-imposed standards and the reasons for this attitude were firmly embedded in the context of the times.

If nineteenth-century society was to avoid breakdown under the strains of developing urbanization, it was urgent to evolve new techniques for enforcing civil discipline. Organized education was part of the answer to this problem. Society was construed as a comity of social ranks, each of which had its place in the whole, and the preservation of society was equated with preservation of those ranks. It was not a question of the state reluctantly intervening in education, whether for the working class or middle class. Maintaining the structure of society meant control and regulation of the ranks of society and this was freely regarded as an essential part of the state's duties, concomitant with civil law and order. As an important agent of control, the educational system was therefore a legitimate state interest. To leave the supply of schools to the market, according to demand, could leave a particular social class with a deficiency of normative facilities; without a system of controls and checks, such schools as were created might also fall short of the standard of social conditioning which they were expected to purvey.

The instructions to Her Majesty's Inspectors issued on 4 July 1840, under the name of the Lord President of Council (Lord Lansdowne), are significant: 'No plan of education ought to be encouraged in which intellectual instruction is not subordinate to the *regulation of the thoughts and habits of the children* by the doctrines and precepts of revealed religion.'[1] 'Regulation of the thoughts and habits of the children' — nothing could have less to do with *laissez-faire*, or be more paternalistic (if not autocratic) than this. Here was the main object of the state in elementary education — to control the thoughts and habits of the labouring poor. The obvious instruments to this end were the churches, but it was the state's responsibility to ensure that the job was properly done.

Lowe is frequently blamed for basing part of his new grant system on examination results and, at the same time, ignoring altogether the Newcastle proposal to increase the number of elementary schools by use of a county rate. Here, it is said, Lowe revealed himself in his true colours as a cheese-paring anti-collectivist, to whom education of the poor meant nothing more than minimal proficiency in reading, writing and arithmetic in a limited number of schools. This must be one of history's most ironic verdicts. The object of the Newcastle Commission's county rate proposal was to make public money available to those church and private schools which were unable to conform to the conditions under which state aid was awarded and so failed to qualify for government grant. The state's conditions, on the other hand, were designed as a guarantee that public money should be funnelled only to responsible bodies who could be trusted not only to discharge the academic requirements of education but also to form the 'thoughts and habits' of the children according to acceptable principles. For this purpose, it was a condition of grant that schools had to be in connection with a religious denomination or provide for the daily reading of the scriptures and also had to be in the charge of a state-certified teacher. The Newcastle Commission would have abandoned those safeguards. Whilst agreeing that existing grant conditions were wise and should continue to apply to exchequer aid, the commissioners proposed that locally levied money should be paid over on the results of examination in the Three Rs to any school which conformed to some very rudimentary building standards, with scarcely any reference to the school's moral atmosphere, to the influence of the schoolmaster or to the general arrangements and course of instruction.

Rate assistance was to be prize money for secular achievement and could be won by private as well as church schools. Historians seem to have forgotten that it was the Newcastle Commission, not Robert Lowe, which said:

> assistance given by the state to education should assume the form of a bounty paid upon the production of certain results by any person whatever. We consider it unfair to exclude the teachers of private schools from a share in this bounty, if they can prove that they have produced the result.[2]

It was Lowe who refused to hand public money to 'any person whatever'. To have done so would, indeed, have established a kind of free trade in education, but in this instance it was Lowe who insisted on a measure of protection. The Newcastle proposal would have abrogated the main object for which parliament voted grants — namely, to ensure that children were not merely intellectually instructed but were subject to a total atmosphere conducive to right moral and social discipline. The government for which Lowe spoke had no doubt that to offer rewards for intellectual success without safeguarding moral tone would lead to a general decline in character-training. It refused to be moved from its policy of supporting and working through agencies — and only those agencies — which had an objectively assessed capacity to carry through the state's 'civilizing' mission. When it became clear that the will and the resources of the sects were inadequate to perform this role to the degree that was needed, the state created additional trustworthy and publicly-controlled agencies — the school boards — to fill the gaps.

Lowe, then, continued a paternalistic policy; but was he not, nevertheless, an economist and the author of a system designed to reduce educational expenditure? As most textbooks point out (following, I suspect, Bartley's analysis, made in 1871 [3]) the amount of parliamentary grant declined in the years following the introduction of the Revised Code and this fact has become the basis of the belief that in 1862 the state tried to contract out of its financial commitment to education, using payment on results as the means by which to effect its escape. Lowe and his colleagues could, of course, have been both paternalistic in attitude and parsimonious in practice, but the effect of the former would be nullified by the latter; such schizophrenia is so remarkable as to require closer examination.

First of all, what effect was the payment on results system likely to have on the exchequer grant? It can be said at once that the government made no change in one of the main principles on which it had paid grant since 1833 — that the annual disbursement should not be a sum fixed beforehand by policy decision, but should be geared to local demand. Textbooks point out (and students tirelessly reiterate in almost every essay on this period) that the first government allocation of £20,000 to education in 1833 was only one-tenth of the sum voted in the same year for repairing the royal stables. But this was not necessarily evidence of educational miserliness in high places. The education grant was to be 50 per cent of the cost of new schools built by the denominations; the total charge falling on the government depended, therefore, on the number and value of projects initiated by the denominations. In order to meet its part of the offer, the Treasury had to make provision for it in its estimates. In arriving at the figure of £20,000 it had regard both to the volume of school building which the National and British Societies had undertaken in recent years, and also to an estimation of what they were likely to build in the coming year. As the amount of building subsequently expanded, so the annual exchequer subsidy increased. Grants for other educational purposes, in 1846 and later, were based on the same principle: the exchequer simply met an agreed proportion of costs incurred not by itself, but by the schools. The Revised Code contained the same feature. It committed the government to payments based on whatever average attendance and whatever number of examination passes could be achieved by those schools which were on its approved list. The charge which fell on central funds as a result of this system could not be foreseen; the only way in which the exchequer could have affected the total call made upon it was by manipulating the unit amounts offered in the grant formula and the conditions under which those amounts were payable. Fiscally, payment by results was itself nothing more than a variation of previous grant conditions, without alteration of the principle of open-ended payment, which persisted (through a variety of further changes in grant conditions) until 1958. That best-known quotation in all educational history − 'If the system is expensive it will at least be efficient; if it is not efficient it will at least be cheap' − expresses not so much a cynical desire to reduce educational costs as a feeling of exasperation at a system which placed the exchequer at the mercy of an outside spender; it was akin to Winston Churchill's complaint in 1926 that the exchequer's only function in local government expenditure was to calculate the price of the tune called by the local authorities.

The global demand made upon government resources was, therefore, just as unpredictable under the new system as it had been before. Did the new grant formula, however, contain some built-in factor which would automatically reduce the amount which schools received? Under the Revised Code each child could, theoretically, earn up to 12s. annually for his school; was this figure realistic and how had it been arrived at?

The Newcastle Commission, which preceded the introduction of the Revised Code, had given considerable thought to the question of unit payment. The latest figures available to it indicated that the specific grants which it was proposed to consolidate into a new block grant (and this is what the Revised Code later effected) were running at approximately 10s. per pupil in average attendance. The Commission accepted this as reasonable and suggested that in order to maintain an average 10s., the earnable maximum per child should be fixed at 15s. This was, of course, just a guess.

It is true that in the financial year ending 31 December 1861, the average grant earned per pupil jumped by 15 per cent over the previous year's figure. But even if this had been fully realized by the government in the early months of 1862, when a figure for the new formula was under consideration, the 1861 result was so far out of line with previous experience, and presented a sudden increase of such magnitude, that no government could have accepted it unquestioningly as the basis for future payment. As it was, the government adopted the Newcastle Commission's recommended 10s. average, but took the gamble that this would be achieved by fixing the earnable maximum at 12s., instead of the 15s. suggested by the Commission. In the outcome, neither was precisely right; it would have been surprising if they had been. The 15s. of the Newcastle Commission would have produced an average well above 10s. Lowe's figure produced an average of only 9s., but after five year's experience the earnable maximum was adjusted to 13s. 4d., with additional specific payments for pupil teachers. In other words, there is no reason to suppose that either Lowe or his governmental colleagues had had any intention of reducing the education grant in 1862; on the contrary, the evidence is that they took great care to maintain the level at which grant had been running in recent years, whilst simplifying (and, they believed, improving) its administration.

To sum up, the Revised Code reduced the volume of centralized activity in Whitehall. The number of schools dealt with individually by the central office had trebled in the ten years preceding 1861. In the circumstances, the Kay-Shuttleworth method of making a variety of *ad hoc* grants to each school separately had become unmanageable and further extension under that system was impossible; the Revised Code, which offered each school a block grant calculated on a common formula, was designed to cope with expansion. It also ended the system under which money could be pumped into schools with no viable means of securing that it was spent efficiently or for the purpose for which it was given; money had now to be earned before it was received. At the same time the principle of open-ended subsidy was maintained: the more schools that qualified for grant-aided status the greater the call on the exchequer; the greater the proficiency of the scholars and the better their attendance the more the Treasury would pay. But Treasury support was still reserved for those schools (and only those schools) which provided a satisfactory moral, as well as intellectual, environment. In all this, it is difficult to discern any new *laissez-faire* intention; on the contrary, Lowe's system exuded paternalism.

It is, of course, understandable that the establishment classes should want to control the lower orders, and even that they should use education as an instrument of regulation. When we come to the area of upper- and middle-class schools, however, state intervention is less obviously explicable. Here, it might be thought, was a field where private enterprise and market economy would be self-sufficient; and, of course, there were many − then, as now − who thought they should be.

Let me quote a letter written in 1867 by a senior clerk in the Colonial Office, replying to a proposal to apply public funds to a middle class school in Trinidad:

> I have always thought it questionable whether the taxpayer at large should be made to pay for the education of the rich. It is no doubt of great importance for the poor that the rich should be educated, and if rich colonists would not have their children educated without a school supported from public funds, it might be right that a school for the rich should be so supplied. But it is a remark as old as Adam Smith that this sort of support is the anodyne of educational institutions and that they are only kept aware and alert when their support depends upon their exertions and their customers whom their reputation attracts. [4]

In other words, subsidies are the opium of private enterprise; here is the very essence of *laissez-faire* philosophy.

It is clear, however, that by 1870 the state had already relegated Adam Smith and adopted the alternative put forward − if not supported − in the first part of the Colonial Office reply. Since it was of paramount importance to the equilibrium and advancement of society that the rich − the natural leaders and providers in all walks of life − should be educated as befitted their station, and since they were failing to supply their own schools, it followed that the state must step in. The Taunton Commission had already taken it for granted that secondary education, for girls as well as boys, was, in its own words, a matter of 'public concern', and had made a series of recommendations for state regulation of upper- and middle-class schools. By 1869, the government had introduced legislation in line with those recommendations.

It is a matter for debate whether historians have given proper emphasis to the real significance of the Taunton Report and the 1869 Bill. Almost all who have written on the work of the Taunton Commission, for example, contrive to give the impression, perhaps unwittingly, that the concept of three classes of school to match three upper and middle social classes was the Commission's own brain-child and that, although the idea was sufficiently interesting to merit the passing attention of scholars, it really had little effect on the mainstream of educational development. I think that this popular view requires more examination than it has hitherto received.

In the absence of public intervention, all schools above the elementary were subject to market pressures. These forces applied not only to private and proprietary schools dependent on the price which their customers were willing to pay, but almost equally, as the Taunton Commission itself demonstrated, to schools endowed with an independent income. Inevitably, the supply of schools and the type of work conducted in them followed demand. The Taunton Report did not invent schools for the classes; they existed long before the Commission was appointed. Nor was it novel to believe that the preservation of social ranks above the labouring poor depended on the existence of a satisfactory stock of efficient schools geared to the education and training of the various middle- and upper-class groups. What was new in the 1860s was not the concept, but the state's willingness to devise and create the machinery necessary to convert the idea into reality. This is what the Taunton Commission and 1869 Bill were about.

The question of what institutions should best be established for the regulation of middle-class schools was one to which much thought had already been given. It seems to have been assumed that apparatus would take the familiar paternalistic form of a government department working through agencies. This was the pattern already set in the field of elementary education and, indeed, the Newcastle Commission had suggested, in 1861, that the Privy Council, responsible for elementary schools, should simply extend its activities to other schools. It would, of course, be necessary for grant conditions to be modified to suit the circumstances of the endowed school, and it was also thought that a special method would have to be devised for certificating endowed school teachers; but the general machinery operating in the elementary field could, it was suggested, be employed.

Instead of accepting this proposal (which was, in any case, outside the Newcastle Commission's brief) the government passed the whole issue to a new body, the Taunton Commission. The object of this was twofold: to create a climate of opinion favourable to state intervention above the elementary level and to produce a viable scheme which the state could operate.

In 1869 — that is to say, in little more than a year after receiving the Taunton report — the government tabled a major education bill designed to ensure a sufficient supply of schools catering for the needs of each middle- and upper-class group in all parts of the country and proposing an elaborate complex of statutory institutions (based on the Taunton recommendations) for providing and supervising them. The fact that this bill preceded legislation for elementary education is in itself indicative of the priority which the government gave to state action in schools beyond those for the poor. The full Taunton proposals would have created a new structure in four tiers, each with its own particular responsibilities. Starting at the bottom, the school head was to be charged with maintenance of discipline, with appointment and dismissal of assistant staff, and supervision of teaching methods. Above the head, the governing body would be responsible for financial management, appointment and dismissal of the head, and determination of the curriculum. Next, the country was to be divided into 11 provinces, each with a provincial authority whose function would be to designate the class or grade to which each school was to be assigned, to ensure that the province had a sufficiency of each grade and to decide whether a school should be a boarding or a day school. Fourthly, a Central Council would be responsible to Parliament for co-ordinating the work of the provincial authorities, inspecting schools, examining pupils, examining and certificating teachers, keeping a register of teachers and presenting an annual report. The 1869 Bill dropped the Provincial Councils and added another body, the Endowed Schools Commissioners, for the purpose of carrying out an initial rationalization of endowments. It was envisaged that this work could be completed in some three years, after which the task of keeping the revised pattern of endowments under review would pass to the Central Council. In the event, the 1869 Act set up only the temporary body of Endowed Schools Commissioners, but in withdrawing the other proposals from his bill, Forster made it clear that he was postponing rather than abandoning them; legislation to deal with them would be re-introduced in about three years' time when the Endowed Schools Commissioners had reconstituted the finances of the schools and provided the provincial and central councils with a base from which they could operate effectively.

It is not my purpose to write the history of this period but only to suggest that there is little evidence here of government aversion to intervention. The meticulous systematization of middle-class schools, envisaged by the Taunton Commissioners and embodied in the 1869 Education Bill, parallels the detail in the 1862 Revised Code for elementary education. We have come, during the twentieth century, to regard education as a social dynamic and to equate increased state activity in it as progress; but the activists of the 1860s were not necessarily looking beyond the society they knew; much of the call for greater state participation in education arose, indeed, from a simple desire to preserve and bring out the best in each social rank by soaking it in its appropriate ethos. For this purpose, different types of school were needed. Society had its greatest success with the upper classes and the public schools. It was fairly successful in the elementary field. That the state failed to move quickly enough to foster sufficient satisfactory schools for the middle classes before the pattern of society itself broke up was due, very largely, to the context in which it had chosen to work. State paternalism, operating deviously through agents, is not the most direct way of achieving an objective; the father-role has its own trials and difficulties. The churches in both elementary and secondary education, and the universities, governing bodies and headmasters in middle-class education, were not the easiest of partners. The state advised, exhorted and offered assistance, but left initiative in private hands. The chosen agents quarrelled amongst themselves, and the state had to be extremely careful how it apportioned its favours. Even more seriously, they frequently reacted against state intervention with all the self-righteousness of adolescents in rebellion against a parent. But, of course, they were not adolescents; they formed some of the most powerful pressure groups in the country, and politicians, coming from the same social class, were rarely ready to apply a heavy hand. This was a situation which was not peculiar to education. Much of our history, in all fields, turns on the ambivalence of sectional interests which need the protection and support of organized society, and even accept its money, but which, at the same time, for reasons of profit or privilege, cling avidly to private power and resent the interference which they themselves invoke; they take what society offers but carry on a love-hate dialogue with the community; they want to remain petty baronies within the state and regard conditions on which they accept public aid as infringements of their own liberty. We are familiar with the forty years' delay in achieving a national system of elementary education, brought about by the unwillingness of the sects to surrender their freedom to the state, whilst carrying on their own internecine war. There has been less study of the forty years' delay in establishing a system of secondary schools, but it is likely that there is a strong parallel between the two stories; the sectional interests which the state hoped to prod into providing an efficient system of middle-class schools wanted the order which could only come from public regulation, but refused to sacrifice their private rights. And the state, for its part, was reluctant to coerce them because it is rarely advisable to bludgeon powerful interests, particularly if they belong to your own class. This, after all, is the secret of the stability of British government.

Professor S. H. Beer, of Harvard, sees the Education Act of 1870, at the end of the decade, as a leading instance of what he calls the 'drift from *laissez-faire*', associated with increasing 'radical' influence on policy. 'Radical' policy, he suggests, involved specific, exceptional acts of state intervention in order to provide a service or to correct particular undesirable consequences of the free economy. Unlike later 'collectivist' policy, it was not an effort to reshape the economic system or to alter its foundations [5]. This, I think, is fair comment — with the rider that the state had rarely been *laissez-faire* in education. I know that there is a familar textbook bromide to the effect that the nineteenth century abhorred government. But the belief that the less government the better was never intended to be applied to the field of civil discipline. This is why I find little difference in spirit between the Education Act of 1870 and events which took place over the preceding years. State intervention was indeed radical and not collectivist; but throughout the 1860s its motivation was anxiety to control, to regulate and to promote. In dealing with the social order the paternal syndrome was stronger than economic principle.

What I am trying to say is probably just this: directly or indirectly, the state has normally been interventionist in education because it is one of the prime objects of government to prevent the breakdown of society, and one of the main instruments for accomplishing this objective is education. The common interpretation of nineteenth-century educational history, which sees a reluctant state dragged into participation by events and pressures, should, perhaps, be turned the other way round: the state was willing enough; it was the difficulty of harnessing churchmen and academics to the task which caused delay.

Notes

[1] Minutes of the Committee of Council on Education, 1840–1.
[2] Report of the Commissioners appointed to inquire into the State of Popular Education in England (the Newcastle Report), vol. 1, p. 96 (B.P.P. 1861, XXI).
[3] G. C. T. Bartley, *The Schools for the People*, 1871.
[4] Minute of Henry Taylor, in Gov. Gordon to Sec. of State, No. 72, 24 May 1867, P.R.O., C.O. 295/239, quoted in E. A. Furlonge, Secondary Education in Trinidad and Tobago, unpublished Ph.D. thesis, p. 110, University of Sheffield, 1968.
[5] S. H. Beer, *Modern British Politics*, Alfred A. Knopf, New York, 1965.

PETER GOSDEN

Technical instruction committees

It is strange that the technical instruction committees should have attracted — and should continue to attract — little attention among historians for it was in these committees that the seeds of future development lay. The growth of technical instruction committees provided the pattern on which the present local education authority was to be modelled by Morant in 1902.

The reconstruction and reform of local government before the 1880s had been confined to the urban communities. The counties remained entirely unreformed, great yawning chasms in the reformed system of local government that was being created in the boroughs. The absence of nation-wide coverage by multi-purpose local government machinery led to the need to create *ad hoc* bodies for each function which had to be dealt with at the local level. The position has been neatly described by Dr Kitson Clark [1].

> Presiding over that life were the country gentry; in the first half of the century in many districts the main source of governmental power. The correspondence of Graham, the Home Secretary, with Peel as Prime Minister and the Duke of Wellington during the troubles of 1842 and 1843 shows how much the government at that moment felt that they depended on the vigour and staunchness of the local magistrates and how important it seemed to them that the country gentry should interest themselves in the work of the Bench and Quarter Sessions and so retain their 'natural influence' in the counties. After 1850 times were quieter, and possibly the successive governments did not need the co-operation of the gentry so urgently. Various counties developed rural police forces; indeed after 1856 they were universal. As new administrative needs were developed for the rural areas they were handed over to elective *ad hoc* bodies and not entrusted to magistrates in Quarter Sessions. But the fact that the cumbrous network of separate districts for different services was developed was possibly partly covered by an unwillingness completely to dispossess the old government of the county in favour of a general elective body; while as far as the rural police were concerned, it seems that at times the gentry who were magistrates found it difficult to remember that they were not also their servants.

More specifically in the field of education, the Taunton Report of 1868 had drawn attention to the need for new local machinery and, in fact, outlined a scheme of provincial government based on existing boards of guardians which might be joined on a county basis into county boards of education which would work under a new central authority presided over by a Minister of Secondary Education.

Nearly twenty years later, the Royal Commission on Technical Instruction, in its Second Report of 1884 suggested that to meet the deficiencies in the provision of secondary and technical education 'it will be necessary to look, in the main, to local resources for any large addition to the funds required for the further development of technical education in this country' [2]. It added, 'It is to be desired that in the proposed re-organization of local government, power should be given to important local bodies, like the proposed county boards and the municipal corporations, to originate and support secondary and technical schools in conformity with the public opinion, for the time being, of their constituents.' [3]

The setting up of county and county borough councils in 1888 may be said to represent the beginning of an attempt to move towards a more rational multi-purpose local authority and away from the system of appointing *ad hoc* bodies for each task that arose — each with its own form of membership and method of election and each with its own pattern of administrative area, e.g. boards of guardians, sewer boards, select and open vestries, etc., as well as school boards. Within a year some educational powers were conferred on the new multi-purpose bodies and I think it is more reasonable to regard this as a step in the new direction of developing the multi-purpose authority rather than to see technical instruction committees as an example of a further proliferation of nineteenth-century *ad hoc* bodies.

The Technical Instruction Act of 1889 was adoptive; it only came into effect if actually adopted by a local authority [4]. It permitted county, borough and urban sanitary authorities to supply or aid the supply of technical instruction to the extent of the product of a 1*d*. rate; these authorities were also permitted to appoint a committee wholly or partly chosen from their own members to carry out their functions under the Act, except for the power of raising a rate or borrowing money which had to be reserved to the parent body. Among other conditions imposed by the Act, the authorities were bound to appoint one or more representatives to the governing bodies of institutions receiving aid, and no aid might be given to public elementary schools, nor to any institution which did not accept a conscience clause. This last condition was inserted by way of amendment in the Commons to appease what might be called the 'school board lobby' who were, however, unsuccessful in their efforts to obtain a share of the new 'technical rate' for the school boards. The central oversight of any arrangements made was given to the Science and Art Department which interpreted its sphere to include inspection in virtually all subjects with the exception of classics and literature.

There was no rush on the part of local authorities to adopt the Act, but several of the larger authorities did take action. The West Riding, for instance, appointed a strong hybrid-type committee 'with a view to bringing the Technical Instruction Act into operation in the West Riding'. Sheffield county borough granted £4,534 in all to Sheffield Technical School, School of Art and the Church Institute. Nottingham, Cardiff, Blackburn, Bolton, York, Worcester and Birkenhead made grants to existing institutions. Many other large authorities were reported by July of 1890 to be considering what action they should take. This group included Birmingham, Leeds, Liverpool, Southampton and Newcastle [5].

If action was to be more than gradual some boost was needed to encourage the authorities to move. A circular of 5 June 1890 from the Science and Art Department tried to provide some stimulus by offering grants in aid of subjects not already grant-aided through its Directory up to the amount voted locally from the rates. An overall limit of £5,000 was imposed, so it was unlikely to achieve a great deal, although the Department itself claimed: 'A new motive is thus supplied to localities to avail themselves of the Act, so as not to be deprived of their share of the grant given to meet local contributions.'

The measure which really injected vigour into local support for technical instruction was the Local Taxation (Customs and Excise) Act of 1890 [6]. This raised the duty on beer and spirits to provide compensation for the extinction of licences, for police pensions and for a general purpose residue to be distributed to county and county borough councils in proportion to their rateable values. Under pressure in the Commons, the government declined to compel councils to spend the residue on education; but at a later stage the licensing provisions were dropped and thus two-thirds of the cash became 'residue' and it did accept a clause which stated, 'the council of any such county or county borough may contribute any sum received by such council in respect of the residue under this section, not exceeding a moiety of the residue or any part of that moiety, for the purposes of technical education within the meaning of the Technical Instruction Act, 1889, and may make such contribution over and above any sum that may be raised under that act.' Thus the county and county borough councils got £743,000 in the first year in England and Wales but were not obliged to spend it on technical education; the whole of the sum could be applied in relief of the rates if so desired. But was the new money to be regarded as permanent income or was it merely a temporary windfall? Clearly this would have a considerable effect on the willingness of authorities to commit themselves to regular expenditure. The National Association for Technical and Secondary Education had a question asked in the Commons on this point. Mr Goschen, the Chancellor of the Exchequer, replied that 'if county councils set themselves heartily to work, as in many places they appear to be doing, to utilize the grants for important educational purposes, it would probably be difficult for any minister to persuade Parliament to divert them, even if he desired so to do.' [7] The National Association naturally encouraged the county councils to support education and did a great deal to help them enter this field by offering sound and useful advice on ways of making the most of their opportunities.

The third piece of legislation instrumental in creating the technical instruction committees as they operated in the 1890s was the Technical Instruction (Amendment) Act of 1891 [8]. This was sponsored by the National Association to remove doubtful points in existing legislation and to deal with some practical difficulties. For instance, it permitted technical instruction committees to aid institutions not situated geographically in their own area and to offer scholarships and exhibitions to students wishing to attend schools and colleges outside their boundaries. The importance of this was considerable, especially in the counties, as may be seen from the following figures which show the position among county councils in the year 1900–1.

19 out of 40 councils providing scholarships to secondary schools permitted them to be held in out-county schools.
31 out of 33 councils providing scholarships to universities and other higher education institutes permitted them to be held outside the county.
31 out of 40 councils providing scholarships in dairy and farming institutes permitted them to be held outside the county. [9]

The general effect of the legislation was that by 1891 the whole country was now completely covered by county and county borough multi-purpose authorities empowered to take action to fill the gaps in the educational provision left by the various specialist agencies and *ad hoc* bodies such as the school boards, the churches and voluntary societies, Science and Art Department classes, trusts and endowments. The gap which appeared to the public to be the most obviously important was in provision for technical education; the more vocal section of the public was most sympathetic to this, hence the gap-filling agencies for education were described as technical instruction committees and were initially aimed principally at meeting this need. But in practice the committees could, did, and often found they had to go beyond technical instruction and act as providers or aiders of all forms of secondary and higher education. So often it proved to be impossible to give technical instruction successfully to pupils whose general level of – or even complete absence of – secondary education rendered them incapable of profiting from such instruction. H. Macan, chief officer to Surrey Technical Instruction Committee, put it like this [10]:

> When the State interferes with a view to equipping its citizens with such knowledge as will fit them to meet foreign competition, the ideal is principally industrial, and aims at making efficient the merchant and the workman ... a good secondary education is not only a necessary supplement to, but the very basis of, a sound technical education in all its higher branches.

Thus if only to make their strictly technical work effective, the counties and county boroughs were forced into the field of secondary education. Some took little persuading while others were more reluctant. It often depended on the attitude of their chief officer. The Bryce Commission, of course, declared technical and secondary education 'inseparable'.

In setting up a form of structure and organization which would enable them to make use of their new educational powers and financial resources, counties and county boroughs had little by way of precedent to guide them. By 1896 the committee and administrative structure had settled down and in 29 county boroughs for which particulars are available only 5 technical instruction committees were composed exclusively of councillors. The other 24 committees had a hybrid membership: in 9 of these, non-members of the council formed a majority. Thus so far as there was a usual pattern in the county boroughs it was for a majority of councillors to sit with a minority of co-opted outsiders – the pattern that was to be followed after 1902.

Such hybrid committees were less usual in the counties. In 1895 only 7 out of 49 counties had technical instruction committees which included non-council members. These were Buckinghamshire (20 council and 6 co-optees), Devon (24 and 2), Essex (24 and 6), London

(20 and 15), Somerset (15 and 12), Wiltshire (17 and 10), and the West Riding (25 and 5). The London technical instruction committee's 15 co-optees included 1 from the I.A.H.M., 1 from the N.U.T., 3 from the City and Guilds Institute, 2 from the London Parochial charities, 3 from the London Trades Council, 3 from London School Board and 2 non-council members nominated by the L.C.C. itself. Some counties without co-opted members on their technical instruction committee nevertheless co-opted outsiders to sub-committees. This was the position in Northumberland and Derbyshire. The total size of the membership of technical instruction committees varied from 20 to 66 [11].

The larger proportion of hybrid committees in the county boroughs may have been due to the representation accorded to coterminous school boards many of which were charged with the provision of certain forms of technical instruction by the local authorities and aided with funds to provide these services. There are certainly many examples of joint action by school boards and technical instruction committees. In 1898—9, the boards received a total of £14,400 in annual grants towards the cost of the higher education services that they laid on. Most of the largest annual grants were made by county borough councils to their coterminous boards as in Leeds (£1,920), Bradford (£1,600), Manchester (£1,500), Hanley and Liverpool (£800). The West Riding County Council distributed £2,000 among 40 boards in the Riding towards the cost of maintaining evening continuation schools and Science and Art classes [12].

In 28 county boroughs the council and the school board had tried to establish their educational arrangements on a comprehensive basis by adopting lines of delimitation or co-ordination or by appointing composite committees. In Bristol, for instance, the technical instruction committee brought together the Society of Merchant Venturers and the School of Art in a scheme to unify evening work. There was an agreement between the Association of Municipal Corporations and the School Boards Association that where joint committees were set up they should be constituted on the basis of the council appointing half of the members and the school board one-third — the remaining sixth would be co-opted. These proportions were often followed, as in Blackburn and Liverpool, but it was not unusual for representatives of the council to be much more numerous than those of the board as in Bristol and Bradford [13].

In a few county boroughs members of the nearby county council sat on the borough technical instruction committee. This was the position in Blackburn, Bradford, Brighton, Chester, Middlesborough, Nottingham, Plymouth, Stockport and Worcester. The reason for such membership was the use of and partial payment for facilities situated in the county borough by the surrounding county area.

Under the Education Act of 1902 local authorities were required to ensure that some women were put on their education committees. A parliamentary return of 1901 showed that 6 counties and 9 county boroughs were already doing this under the existing technical instruction legislation, while another 13 authorities co-opted women members to their sub-committees. Even so, the total number of women members was not large — it amounted to 153 in the whole of England and Wales.

The great majority of local authorities delegated all of their educational powers under the Acts to their technical instruction committees with the exception of the power to raise a rate or to borrow money. These two reserved powers were, of course, those which later came to be reserved from the education committee to the council itself under the 1902 Act.

The structure of sub-committees varied greatly from one authority to another depending largely on the balance of local political and social influences. In some counties much of the work was passed over to local committees, as in Lancashire where the central technical instruction committee was quite remarkably lame and unenterprising. The reverse of this was to be seen in Surrey, the West Riding and London. Thus it is not possible to describe arrangements in a typical county because there was no such place. A county in which so many local committees were established that the work of technical instruction was gravely impeded was Dorset where no fewer than 53 local administrative units were created to meet the needs of a small and scattered population. I have already described the position in that county elsewhere [14]. A county not entirely dissimilar in its social and economic pattern to Dorset was Somerset. Here a determined attempt was made to balance the local and county interests, to make full use of local enthusiasm and knowledge while also benefiting from the greater measure of expertise and superior organization which the larger unit could offer. Somerset owed a great deal to the personal influence of Henry Hobhouse who was a powerful figure on its technical instruction committee. He justified the county's arrangements in 1892 in these words [15]:

> Our problem being to bring instruction as near as possible to the doors of the people in each village, we gain more than we lose by multiplying district and local committees. Of course there are drawbacks in this particularism: more clerks to pay, more correspondence and printing, difficulties in finding teachers, a want of uniformity

and a variety of experiment, alarming to the mind of the systematic organizer. But, on the whole, the money is being well-spent, and everyone, from the schoolboy or dairy maid up to the county councillor himself, is gaining knowledge and experience by the new movement, whether it be in the elements of science and art, or in organization and local government.

The central technical instruction committee consisted of 15 members of the council and 12 co-opted members, two of whom were women. There were sub-committees at the centre for agricultural instruction, mining, scholarships, cookery, teachers' classes and peripatetic lectures. The annual income of £12,000 was divided into three parts. Firstly a County Fund of £4,000 to cover office expenses, university extramural lectures and teachers' classes, also to support schools and other institutions considered to be of value to the whole county. Secondly £5,000 was allocated to a District Fund which was divided among local committees in each Poor Law Union district on a population basis. Thirdly £3,000 was paid into a District Reserve Fund for scholarships and for securing by grant aid a fuller utilization of educational endowments of district importance.

The arrangements in Somerset might be compared with those in Surrey or London. The chairman of the London Technical Instruction Board (as it called itself) was Sydney Webb, and at the first meeting of the Board a sub-committee was appointed to consider organization and procedure. This recommended that all business should be handled in sub-committees reporting to the Board. Work was to be divided among the sub-committees on a functional basis which meant that sub-committee members often acquired a measure of expertise from their experience. This contrasted strongly with the position in counties relying heavily on local committees, for at the local level there was often insufficient business of one type to make it worthwhile setting up sub-committees of local committees and, at the same time, there was not enough work in any one field to give local members anything like the experience of any particular class of business that a county level sub-committee member would acquire.

The resources available to technical instruction committees consisted mainly of the Residue Grant, occasionally supplemented from the rates. Although the Residue Grant did not have to be spent on education, much of it was from the start. By 1897 only 8 counties and 6 county boroughs were using part of it for the general relief of rates. By 1902 the number of counties applying part of it in this way was reduced to 7 and the number of county boroughs to 3, while 105 counties and county boroughs were devoting the whole of the Grant to education. For the financial year 1900–1 the Residue Grant amounted to £1,028,000; in the same year the total amount raised by rating for technical education was £128,534 – or about one-eighth of the total sum available by grant. Rates had been levied by 31 per cent of the authorities with some technical instruction powers, by 351 out of 1,121 councils, for while the Residue Grant went only to counties and county boroughs, non-county boroughs and urban districts could raise a rate for technical instruction if they so desired. A number of counties had levied rates on certain parts of their areas with the assent of the minor authority in order to help a local secondary or technical school, but only Surrey and the West Riding levied education rates on the whole of their administrative areas before the Act of 1902 [16].

The manner of disbursing the resources available again presented a very varied picture and few general statements can be made. But it would certainly be true to say that in the early years much more was spent on lectures than in later years while there was a steady increase in the proportion of available funds spent on secondary schools and on scholarships to these schools and to institutions of higher education.

In the early years inexperience led to a concentration of funds on paying for technical or scientific lectures by extramural lectures to those lacking the general educational background which would have enabled them to benefit from them. There are many examples of this; Shropshire's scheme in the year 1890–1 for the distribution of its resources may be taken as typical. The total available was £6,260 and it was divided thus:

	£
Travelling lecturers	2,790
Cooking and laundry classes	1,000
Urban authorities (grants based on rateable values)	800
Cheese- and butter-making classes	500
Expenses of organization	420
Science and Art classes in Shrewsbury, Oswestry and Wellington	300
Scholarships to secondary schools	200
Lectures on agriculture for teachers	100
Scholarships to higher education institutions	100
Scholarships for dairymaids	25
Scholarships for cooks	25

The increasing realization of the need to concentrate more finance on general secondary and higher education and the possibility of actually doing this because of the very wide interpretation the Science and Art Department put on the word 'technical' led to a steady growth in the number of scholarships offered, to an increase in grants to endowed grammar schools and to more grants to institutions of higher education. By 1899, only 17 authorities were not operating a system of scholarships to grammar schools. There was usually a limit on parental incomes

TABLE I

A comparison of scholarships awarded in counties and county boroughs in 1894 and 1899 [18]

Scholarships tenable in	Number in 1894	Number in 1899	Total Cost 1894	1899
Evening classes	3,445	4,556		
Technical and Art Schools	419	2,424		
Secondary Schools	1,730	2,485		
Universities and Colleges	267	297	£56,470	£80,652
Agricultural Colleges	299	436		
Domestic Economy Classes	244	1,128		
Elementary Teacher Training	2,304	1,599		

for the award of scholarships although the Science and Art Department ruled that there need not be one: Liverpool imposed a limit of £250, Somerset £400, Northumberland £200 – the lowest was Hanley (£150) and the highest Manchester (£500). By comparison with school awards, scholarships to universities and colleges were very few in number, only 297 in 1899. Here, again, the more active authorities were the more generous. London offered 40 awards which lasted for three years, and were worth £60 plus free tuition each year. Hereford offered one award of up to £60 with free tuition for two years. These awards were often tied to particular institutions. The Isle of Wight, for instance, offered two awards both of which were tenable only at the Hartley College, Southampton while Cheshire's scholarships were tenable only at Liverpool, Manchester and Aberystwyth. Cornwall and Cumberland were among the counties offering no awards.

Direct aid to existing schools and other institutions was either based on a recurrent grant as a contribution towards maintenance and running costs or took the form of a special grant for such a purpose as building a new laboratory. Where grant was given, the technical instruction committee was obliged to put at least one member on the governing body of the institution so aided. Grants were widely used by the more enterprising authorities to put new life into old endowments. The new life was often ensured not only by obtaining representation on the governing body but also by attaching carefully drawn conditions to the grant, possibly requiring that a school should be open to inspection by the authority's inspectors or that its curriculum be revised. The West Riding was very active in this respect and created a fairly complete system of secondary education which was fully described in the Bryce Report by the Assistant Commissioner. The university colleges sometimes benefited directly from technical instruction money — Manchester paid Owens College £1,000 per annum.

Occasionally an authority used a considerable proportion of its resources to build up a particular institution. This was the case at Southampton. Hartley College was founded with what was left of Henry Robinson Hartley's bequest after costly litigation and it was opened by Palmerston in 1862. The college really offered little but Science and Art Department courses, but in 1889 it applied for a share in the first Treasury grant to the universities. The early version of the University Grants Committee rejected the claim 'as there is not a professorial staff adequate for the complete teaching of university subjects'. The College Council, advised by Sir Philip Magnus, set about raising standards and to help it obtained a grant of £700 per annum from Southampton's share of the Residue Grant along with the proceeds of a ½d. rate in the town. Hampshire paid a grant of £75 annually and from these sources a total annual income of £4,000 materialized. The teaching staff was reorganized and increased; new buildings were put up, partly with special additional aid from Hampshire. Hampshire, the Isle of Wight, Dorset and Wiltshire tied scholarships to the College and there was hope by the end of the nineteenth century of its being recognized for Treasury grant [19].

To aid an existing institution, even to the point of changing it beyond recognition, is one thing; but to found an entirely new secondary grammar school was much more difficult under the limited powers conferred by the Technical Instruction Acts. It was just possible, however, and it did happen. In spite of all the difficulties involved, Surrey showed sufficient enterprise to establish four county grammar schools. One of these was Richmond County School. The technical instruction committee proposed to grant £4,000 towards the erection of a school at Richmond and the town council voted £1,250 as a contribution to the cost of the building. A site was purchased near the railway station and therefore convenient for pupils from Kew, Mortlake and Barnes. The foundation stone was laid by the Duke of Cambridge on 24 July 1895 and the school was opened in the following year. It was governed by a body of 21 members which included 4 members *ex officio* (the chairman and vice-chairman of the County Council, the mayor and the vicar of Richmond), 8 members appointed by Surrey County Council, 5 by Richmond Borough Council and 1 each by University College, King's College, the City and Guilds Institute and the I.A.H.M. Surrey pupils were charged a fee of £6 per annum and ex-county pupils £10. The Surrey technical instruction committee contributed an annual grant of £450 and provided the services of a modern languages master. Grants earned mainly by pupils' examination successes from the Science and Art Department amounted to £400 in 1897–8. The actual cost of the education given worked out at about £12 for each boy annually. The school was organized in six forms: the four most senior constituted a school of science for grant purposes; both French and German were taught in the upper forms and French alone in the lower. Over a third of the pupils were drawn from elementary schools, 75 per cent were resident in Richmond and 11 per cent travelled in from Middlesex daily. Surrey awarded 15 scholarships to the school annually and more were offered by local trusts. By 1901, 4 pupils had gained County Major awards and were at University and King's Colleges. An extension needed to be added to the building very soon after the school was opened so that the total capital cost amounted to £12,910: £9,630 of this was provided by Surrey technical instruction committee, £2,800 by the borough of Richmond, £500 by the Science and Art Department and £280 by private subscribers [20].

Quite as important for the future as these achievements was the emergence of the occupation of educational administrator at the county level and the building up of a body of professional expertise and knowledge. The injection of the Residue Grant into technical instruction meant that large funds became immediately available and had to be administered. This administration was a complicated business and special machinery was obviously necessary in the counties to deal with it. Initially such machinery was not so obviously necessary in the county boroughs where much of the money was passed on to the coterminous school board organization to support higher grade schools and evening classes. Most counties appointed a full-time officer to take charge of their technical instruction work.

The Association of Organizing Secretaries and Directors for Secondary and Technical Education was founded in 1891 and the great majority of officers joined this. The Association was from the start far more concerned with educational questions than with the narrower occupational issues such as salary matters: it was not primarily a trade union. An examination of the annual reports gives some idea of the main business. The report for 1901, a typical year, showed that there had been eight meetings and that the matters considered at some length included the representation on joint scholarship boards of each authority using a board's examinations, the Higher Elementary School Minute, the Society of Arts Scheme for examinations in commerce, increase in government grants to smaller schools of science, use of London Matriculation results for the award of intermediate scholarships, representation of teachers on technical instruction committees and representations to government departments on a whole series of educational issues [21]. The Association has since become the Association of Education Officers.

The great controversies provoked by the proposals of the 1902 Act to make county and county borough councils all purpose L.E.A.s must be viewed against this background of considerable educational activity and achievement by those councils. So far as technical, secondary and higher education were concerned, the Education Act of 1902 placed them all on the same footing and repealed the Technical Instruction Acts while continuing the 'whisky money' arrangement, the whole of which had now to be spent on 'education other than elementary' – still the only positively definable area. County and county borough councils were also empowered to raise a rate for these purposes; counties, but not county boroughs, were limited to a 2*d*. rate – before levying more they had to get the permission of the Local Government Board.

There is still a fairly widespread belief, possibly fostered by a few of the more abbreviated type of student texts in use, that the Education Act of 1902 marked the entry of the county councils into the local educational scene. But it is clear that the technical instruction committees were far more than shadowy forerunners of the 1902 L.E.A.s. The more closely one examines the structure, organization and scope of the work of the counties under the Technical Instruction Acts, the less significant a watershed does 1902 appear to be. In many counties it was a matter of a machine already there and operating smoothly, extending its operation to include the oversight of the elementary field. The controversies of 1902 were rightly centred on the elementary schools where the true innovations lay. In 1902 the government's choice between *ad hoc* school board or county-based systems was no doubt conditioned largely by political factors; but any administration would have found itself faced with a choice between a nation-wide and fairly well organized county-board machine and a system which catered for only some parts of the country, some of which it served very well – for example, the great cities – but some of which it served very indifferently.

Students of the development of local educational administration find the 1890s the most exciting because it was the most formative decade. The 1902 concept of a local education authority was based on the best practice evolved by many counties and county boroughs in the 1890s and contained its main features. The education committees themselves were to be hybrid bodies consisting mainly of members drawn from the council but with co-opted members added from outside. The sub-committee structure, based largely on a functional division of work, had already emerged in many counties. Where local committees had been important in the 1890s they usually survived as area or district committees; the traditions established in this respect showed a remarkable quality of persistence in such counties as Lancashire where the tradition is now reflected in the large number of small divisional executives. The practice of delegating full powers to the education committee, with the reservation only of the powers to raise a rate or to borrow, was the familiar practice before as well as after 1902. Finally, but in one way most important of all, there was the creation of a group of local administrative officers who developed a professional expertise and sense of responsibility in the nineties which prepared them for the wider field which opened after 1902. The success of the Balfour Act owed far more than it is customary to recognize to the creation of this corps of knowledgeable officials by counties under the Technical Instruction Acts.

Notes

[1] G. Kitson Clark, *The Making of Victorian England*, Methuen, 1962, p.222.
[2] *Second Report of the Royal Commission on Technical Instruction*, 1884, vol.I, p. 515.
[3] Ibid., p. 517.
[4] 52 and 53 Vict., c. 76.
[5] *Third Report of the National Association for the Promotion of Technical and Secondary Education*, 1890, p. 11.
[6] 53 and 54 Vict., c. 60.
[7] Hansard 4 Dec. 1890 (in answer to Ld. Hartington).

[8] 54 and 55 Vict., c. 4.
[9] 'The Scholarship Schemes of English County and County Bor-
     ough Councils', *The Record*, x (July 1901), p. 348.
[10] H. Macan, 'The New Official Return Respecting Secondary
     Schools in England', *The Record*, vii (July 1898), p. 302.
[11] The figures relating to committee membership are from the
     *Eighth and Ninth Reports of National Association for the
     Promotion of Technical and Secondary Education*, 1895 and
     1896. The composition of some Technical Instruction Com-
     mittees is also described in the *Report of the Royal Commission
     on Secondary Education*, 1895, I, (Appendix) pp. 420–3.
[12] *County Council Times*, 10 March 1900, p. 132.
[13] Ibid.
[14] P. Gosden, *The Development of Educational Administration in
     England and Wales*, 1966, pp. 157–8.
[15] Henry Hobhouse, 'The Working of the Technical Instruction Acts
     in Somerset', in *Studies in Secondary Education*, 1892, ed. A. H.
     D. Acland and H. Llewellyn Smith, p. 105.
[16] *Fourteenth Report of the National Association for the Pro-
     motion of Technical and Secondary Education*, 1903, p. 31.
[17] *Fourth Report of the National Association for the Promotion of
     Technical and Secondary Education*, 1891, p. 27.
[18] Figures drawn from the *Ninth Report of the National Association
     for the Promotion of Technical and Secondary Education*, 1896,
     pp. 8–9, and from *The Record*, x (July 1901), p. 288.
[19] 'The Hartley College, Southampton', *The Record*, vii (Oct.
     1898), pp. 498–508.
[20] A. E. Backhurst, 'Richmond County School', *The Record*, x
     (July 1901) pp. 363–8.
[21] A brief description of each year's activities was given in the
     relevant *Report of the National Association for the Promotion of
     Technical and Secondary Education*.

LESLIE WYNNE EVANS

The evolution of Welsh educational structure and administration 1881-1921

The forty years between 1881 and 1921 mark, in many ways, a Welsh educational awakening. It was during this period that the main girders were welded together in the evolution of Welsh educational structure and administration. The list of achievements in this brief space of time was most impressive, and apart from the elementary school system which after 1870 evolved on the English national pattern, Wales had acquired a National University, a viable system of intermediate and secondary schools, a Central Welsh Board, a Welsh Department of the Board of Education, a National Library, a National Museum, and, to boot, almost achieved educational autonomy – had the National Council for Education come into being in 1906. It is the evolution of this structure that will be examined here.

On St David's day, 1921, Sir Harry Rudolph Reichel, first Principal of the University College of North Wales, Bangor, said in his address to the Manchester Welsh Society:

> My own experience, extending now over thirty-seven years in Wales, has witnessed a Renaissance period, a time of extraordinary activity, of rapid development and reconstruction. So completely have the mental outlook and social life been transformed, that anyone who had known the Principality before the eighties, and been cut off from all communications with it ever since, would hardly recognize his surroundings if he returned to it now . . . During this period a great system of secondary schools has been established, and the small and struggling college of 1872 has grown into a National University, with four times as many teachers as the original college possessed students. [1]

Reichel should have gone further to include the establishment of the Welsh Department in 1907 and its activities in the formative period up to 1921.

Although 1881 is the starting point of this survey, the year 1868 cannot be ignored nor the events in Wales, especially in the political field, leading up to that year. On the educational side, before 1868, the provision of education for the children of Wales in day schools, whether at elementary or higher levels, was most inadequate apart from the elementary works day schools associated with the various Welsh heavy industries and the Voluntary Societies which were doing excellent work within their limits. The publication of the notorious Blue Books produced by the Education Commissioners of 1847 and called in Wales the 'Treachery of the Blue Books', 'largely nullified the effect of their report through their mass indictment of the culture, social conditions, religion, and morals of the people of Wales' [2]. They did little to improve relations between England and Wales but served to unite Welshmen from one end of the country to the other, and, more important still, brought into the limelight the whole question of Welsh education. Welshmen realized the force of Kay-Shuttleworth's contention that there would never be any real improvement in education until Wales had a good supply of trained teachers. This implied training colleges in the Principality to supplement the already well-known trek of Welsh pupil-teachers to the Borough Road Training College in London which almost became a household word in Wales during the nineteenth century. But Wales had, long before 1870, three or four training colleges such as the Brecon Normal School in 1846 which had a brief life since it depended on voluntary subscriptions; the Church of England training colleges at Trinity College, Carmarthen, and Caernarvon in 1848 and 1849 respectively [3], and Bangor Normal College in 1858. On the so-called secondary side there were a few old grammar schools, e.g. Friars School, Bangor; Cowbridge Grammar School; Queen Elizabeth's Grammar School, Carmarthen, and other endowed schools of more recent origin such as Christ's College, Brecon, and Llandovery College whose first warden was the Venerable John Williams, Archdeacon of Cardigan, who had been for over twenty years Rector of Edinburgh Academy and was described by Sir Walter Scott as a 'Heaven born teacher and the greatest schoolmaster in Europe' [4].

Only three secondary schools were available for girls, Dr Williams's school, Dolgellau, and the Howells' schools at Denbigh and Llandaff. Finally, on the higher education side there was the Church of England College at Lampeter, and some nonconformist academies and denominational theological colleges. At the base there was one pure Welsh educational institution which preserved the Welsh language – the Sunday School. Everyone who wished to do so, attended this school from the cradle to the grave, and well after the Education Act of 1870 until the introduction of compulsory education by Mundella in 1880, Sunday schools were far more popular than day schools [5]. Only the Sunday schools in fact remained a truly Welsh institution, for the system of Welsh intermediate schools after 1889 and the University of Wales were modelled on the older English endowed schools and the Queen's University of Ireland and London University respectively [6].

On the political side the year 1868 was of great significance for Welsh education. Briefly, the 'triumphant elections of 1868 in Wales' after the extension of the franchise in Disraeli's Reform Act of 1867 'symbolized the awakening of the Welsh nation' [7] when nonconformity and political radicalism became synonymous, engendering consciousness of nationhood particularly in the field of higher education after 1880. For the first time Wales had a band of Liberal Members of Parliament at Westminster which in the nineties grew into a vigorous Welsh Parliamentary Party with the two stars Tom Ellis and Lloyd George at the centre. In this same context tribute must be paid to the English friends of Wales in the evolution of the Welsh educational system, such as Gladstone, Lord Spencer, James Bryce and his friend W. T. Warry (one of the Principal Officers of the Charity Commissioners and Secretary of the Aberdare Departmental Committee). Among those in the House of Commons who played a major part were A. J. Mundella, Sir William Hart-Dyke, A. H. Dyke Acland (a close friend of Tom Ellis) and Augustine Birrell, briefly President of the Board of Education − not forgetting two Inspectors of the Board who knew Wales so thoroughly − A. G. Legard and Thomas Darlington, the latter being able to speak Welsh fluently. All these are more than names to any student of Welsh education who studies the records.

We cannot arrive at 1881 without referring to the Education Act of 1870 and the establishment of the University College of Wales at Aberystwyth in October 1872. Legislatively, Wales was merely part of the English elementary school pattern which emerged from Forster's Act, but the main features in Wales were the controversies which arose with regard to Church National schools in 'single school' areas where such schools catered for a nonconformist community and the question of religious instruction which again raised its head after the Balfour Act with the Welsh Defaulting Authorities in 1904. But the opening of the College at Aberystwyth was the spearhead of a national campaign for higher education and became a distinctively Welsh question in the House of Commons evoking 'sympathetic response from both political parties' [8], and led to the establishment of the Departmental Committee of 1880 under the chairmanship of Henry Austin Bruce

(Lord Aberdare) which inquired into the defective condition of intermediate and higher education in Wales.

The population of Wales in 1871 was just under one and a half million and the funds not only for establishing but also for maintaining the College were collected from all over Wales and some English cities, in a campaign organized by Sir Hugh Owen and others. Even a University Sunday was set apart for collections from the Welsh nonconformist chapels [9]. The monetary details are fascinating: nearly £9,000 was raised in three years; 100,000 persons gave sums under 2s.6d.; 5,000 exactly 2s.6d.; 4,000 gave over 2s.6d.; in later years only seven persons had given sums of £1,000, and seven persons from £500 to £1,000 [10]. Right up to 1882 the College depended on voluntary subscriptions for its existence. Two Welsh MPs, Henry Richard and Osborne Morgan failed to persuade Gladstone to sanction government subvention because he was apprehensive about the religious issue and hesitated to commit the State to a new principle in aiding colleges from the Exchequer on the basis of their offering only an undenominational education [11]. But the College started with 25 students and by 1900 there were 1,310 students undergoing courses at the three constituent colleges of the University of Wales. What accounted for the rapid rise in student numbers by 1900? How did Wales obtain three constituent colleges between 1872 and 1884 and a full-blown University of Wales in 1893? These are the questions which must be considered in order to describe the remarkable and rapid developments that took place in Welsh higher education in the brief space of twenty years, from the Aberdare Report of 1881 to the Balfour Act of 1902, which covers the first phase in the evolution of Welsh educational structure and administration. The second phase extends from 1902 up to and including the establishment of the Welsh Department of the Board of Education in 1907, and the third phase from 1907 to the publication of the Bruce report in 1920 on the reorganization of secondary education in Wales.

I

The development of Welsh education shows that history is no respecter of logic. Wales had training colleges before it acquired a national system of elementary schools, and University Colleges before secondary schools. In point of fact Wales was in the singular position of building its educational system from the top instead of from the bottom [12]. Long before 1881 much had been written on Welsh higher education and many meetings had been held by leading Welshmen in London and elsewhere. The first college for higher education was St David's College, Lampeter, founded by Bishop Burgess in 1827 and incorporated by Royal Charter in 1827 'for the reception and education of persons destined for Holy Orders'. For special reasons Lampeter was never merged into the Welsh University until 1967 when arrangements were completed for its incorporation as a constituent institution of the University after a period of sponsorship by University College, Cardiff [13].

Strange to relate, the Welsh University movement was initiated by a body of Welsh clergy ministering in England [14]. In 1852 they petitioned Parliament for 'a University founded on broad and liberal principles to meet the needs of the Welsh people, churchmen or dissenters' [15]. There were other moves, e.g. in 1853, B. T. Williams, a young Glasgow graduate and later MP for Carmarthen, proposed in a pamphlet the idea of a unitary university in one place on the Scottish plan. In 1854, Sir Hugh Owen at a London meeting proposed a Welsh university on the model of the Queen's Colleges in Ireland run on unsectarian lines. The Crimean War intervened, and in 1862 and 1863 further meetings led to the opening of the Aberystwyth college which many thought would become the national university — but this was not to be [16].

There was little purpose in having a university or colleges unless students were forthcoming — above elementary level. Several people had drawn attention to this situation including the Rev. D. Lewis Lloyd, Headmaster of Friars school, Bangor, in his pamphlet published in 1876 [17]. Lloyd was disturbed that the education of the working classes ended with the public elementary school and that 'a vast amount of natural ability existed among the artisan and working classes' which was wasted [18]. He suggested some remedies including schemes for scholarships to be established all over Wales. In 1879, the Member for Glamorgan, H. Hussey Vivian of Swansea, brought the attention of the House to the deficiencies of Welsh higher education. While Ireland had 1,634 students (1 to 3,121 of the population), and Scotland an impressive 4,000 (1 to 840), the total number of Welsh students enjoying higher education of any kind at Jesus College, Oxford, at Lampeter College, and at the newly-fledged college at Aberystwyth was a mere 189, and secondary education was almost non-existent. The twenty-seven Welsh Grammar Schools were largely situated away from the large urban centres swollen by industrial expansion. These schools shared £6,531 annually and their pupils numbered less than 4,000

[19]. The debate 'made Welsh higher education a political issue for the first time' and when Gladstone returned to power he acted quickly [20]. The letters from Gladstone and Lord Spencer to Lord Aberdare (who had proposed an inquiry) and from James Bryce and Mundella to Sir Hugh Owen and others between 10 May and 25 August 1880, describe in detail the establishment of the Aberdare Departmental Committee on intermediate and higher education in Wales [21]. The work was done fully and expeditiously and the Report appeared within a year, on 18 August 1881. This was hailed in the Principality as the educational charter of Wales. It dealt with the educational requirements under four headings [22] :

1. The provision needed for intermediate education;
2. The establishment of provincial colleges;
3. The expediency of creating a degree-giving university in Wales;
4. The sources from which the necessary funds might be obtained.

In Chapter 4 of the Report due attention was paid to the distinct nationality of Wales and it was stated that

> that system of education is most desirable for Wales which while preserving the national type, improves and elevates it, and at the same time gives opportunity for the development of any literary tastes or intellectual aptitudes which may be characteristic of the nation . . . this is, in our opinion, a reason for securing within the limits of Wales itself a system of intermediate and higher education in harmony with the distinctive peculiarities of the country [23].

Mention was also made of the deep religious convictions and the zeal for education of the Welsh people and one witness gave the amazing testimony that in 1875 the Welsh spent no less that £100,000 on Welsh literature of all kinds [24]. Even Hussey Vivian on the night of 14 May 1889 (the night before the second reading of the Intermediate Education, Wales, Bill on 15 May) in the debate on the Established Church in Wales, stated in his speech that 'the Welsh Nonconformists have built their own places of worship and maintain them by expending £300,000 and £400,000 annually' [25]. On the schools side the Report found that the total number of boys in endowed grammar schools, proprietary schools and private schools was 4,036, and maintained that out of a total population of 1,570,000, Wales was entitled to accommodation for 15,700 pupils on a basis of 10 per 1,000 [26].

The Report recommended the creation of a new system of intermediate schools and the establishment of two Colleges, one in south Wales and one in the north — at Aberystwyth, Bangor, or Caernarvon — with a grant of £4,000 a year each [27]. Lampeter College was to be affiliated to them [28]. No recommendation was made for Jesus College, Oxford, nor for the teaching of Welsh [29]. It is significant to note that although the Report acknowledged separate treatment for Wales in the field of higher education it did not mention a national body or council for Wales. It will be seen that this matter reappears more than once before 1907. Nevertheless the Welsh educational structure for the next twenty years emerged from the recommendations of this Report.

Speed was again the keynote in the implementation of the Report's recommendations and strangely enough the order was (a) the establish-ment of two Colleges in 1883 and 1884, (b) the Welsh Intermediate Education Act of 1889, and (c) the University of Wales in 1893. Stranger still, the Welsh intermediate schools appeared after the creation of the Welsh University. A tremendous amount of heat and jealousy was engendered in Wales over the location of the two Colleges, for Aberystwyth was considered too remote to serve the interests of north Wales. The two south Wales contenders were Swansea and Cardiff who presented imposing memorials setting forth their claims. Three arbitrators were called in — Lord Carlingford, A. J. Mundella, and Sir Frederick Bramwell — and Cardiff won the day [30]. The same arbitrators selected Bangor from among thirteen applications in north Wales [31]. The College at Cardiff was opened in 1883, the first Principal being John Viriamu Jones, then aged twenty-seven, son of a Welsh Congregational minister. Formerly principal and professor of physics and mathematics at Firth College, Sheffield, he was a close friend of A. J. Mundella, who was MP for the Brightside division of the city, and a moving spirit in Welsh educational development on every front in subsequent years [32]. The college at Bangor opened in 1884 with H. R. Reichel as Principal [33].

This brought into question the position of Aberystwyth which had been awarded a grant of £4,000 in 1882 as the only existing college [34]. Mundella, Vice-President of the Council in Gladstone's Second Ministry, had to overcome the opposition of some of his colleagues to the recommended grant of £8,000 a year to two Welsh colleges, and this was only approved in 1883 'with the greatest difficulty and by Gladstone's imperative decision' [35]. With half this sum earmarked for Cardiff in the same year and the other half for Bangor in 1884, was the Alma Mater at Aberystwyth to be sacrificed? But Aberystwyth had penetrated too deeply into the affections of the Welsh people to be the object of such summary dismissal. Numerous controversies and objections were swept aside and Mundella once more extracted a further grant of £2,500 for the College. This was raised to £4,000 in 1885 and in 1890 the Salisbury administration granted Aberystwyth its charter as a University College according it equal status with Cardiff and Bangor [36]. Instead, therefore, of the two University Colleges recommended by the Aberdare Report, Wales secured three in less than a decade.

Here, it would not be amiss to digress a little – to dispel any misgivings English people might entertain regarding the temperate inhibitions of the Welsh. It is exciting to find that, notwithstanding the fact that Wales secured an Act in 1881 prohibiting the sale of intoxicating liquors on Sundays, two of her University Colleges started life in hotels, and, moreover, after the passing of the Local Taxation (Customs and Excise) Act of 1890, the appropriation of 'whisky money' (commonly called the Goschen Fund) with such alacrity by the Welsh County Authorities expedited the completion of the Welsh system of intermediate schools [37]. Again, the Central Welsh Board was conceived and born at the Raven Hotel, Shrewsbury – the Welsh academic capital. Even today many university meetings are held in similar hostelries in the same town, whilst innumerable appointments to Chairs in the Welsh University have been filled at the Great Western Hotel, Paddington!

The colleges once established, where were the students to come from? Of the 313 students enrolled at Aberystwyth between 1872 and 1880, 70 were under sixteen years of age and many returned home after one or two terms [38]. At Cardiff, Viriamu Jones, faced with the same problem (entrance requirements were meagre and professors had to impart elementary instruction), was more than ever convinced of the urgent need to develop intermediate education. On the other hand, headmasters of grammar and proprietary schools in South Wales were hostile to what they regarded as a rival institution. Meeting at Shrewsbury in 1885 to form a provisional committee for the protection of the old endowed schools, and to watch the progress of the Intermediate Education Bill for Wales due to come before Parliament, they called for an admission age of seventeen and an entrance examination which 'would effectually protect such colleges from the necessity of undertaking elementary instruction' [39]. But the fears of competition were largely illusory as the majority of students entering the Welsh Colleges in the 1880s could have had no opportunity of secondary school training.

From 1882 to 1889, Mundella proved to be the fairy godmother of Welsh intermediate education. His work throughout was prosecuted in the spirit of a letter he wrote to Viriamu Jones in 1893:

I am well satisfied with the progress of education in Wales. My initiative is working like a little leaven, and I hope when Wales has worked out its own salvation, it will have the effect of leavening the larger and more inert mass of Englishmen. I always desired to see Wales become a model for our national system, and I am increasingly hopeful that it will gradually become so. [40]

But at first there were disappointments. Bills to promote Welsh intermediate education introduced by Mundella in 1882, 1883 and 1885 proved abortive. Two others were mooted in 1887 and 1888 but neither was discussed. One of the stumbling blocks was the question of how intermediate schools should be administered, but with the passing of the Local Government Act of 1888 it could be proposed that the new County Councils should become the local education authorities.

The Parliamentary debates for the session 1889 contain a large chunk of Welsh educational history [41]. It fell to Stuart Rendel, MP for Montgomery, who was successful in a draw for private members' Bills, to conduct the measure for Welsh intermediate education through its second reading in the Commons on 15 May 1889. He had worked in complete harmony with Tom Ellis, MP for Merionethshire, and such English members as Gladstone, Mundella, Hart-Dyke, and Dyke Acland, to bring it to this stage. Rendel pleaded for 'completion of the missing link' and an 'educational ladder' from elementary school to university by establishing a system of intermediate schools, undenominational in character and administered by the new County Councils which should have powers to levy a halfpenny rate backed by an equivalent Treasury grant. The Bill also sought a National Council for Education in Wales [42]. Before the Act was passed certain mutilations were inevitable. Two important deletions were the proposed National Council, thus perpetuating the powers of the Charity Commissioners, and the placing of administrative responsibilities in the hands of local 'county committees' instead of the County Councils [43]. The Act received Royal Assent on 12 August 1889, and at the close of that month the Technical Instruction Act was also passed [44].

The omission of the National Council which would give educational autonomy for Wales was a bitter blow. It is worth probing deeper into the conception of this Council for no topic was discussed in Welsh education so regularly and at times so fanatically between 1889 and 1920 and on every occasion was doomed to failure. The germ of such a Council can be traced back to the Schools Inquiry Commission of the sixties [45]. In the debate on the Welsh Intermediate Education Bill in the House of Commons, Tom Ellis said:

this proposal for a Board of Education for Wales is no new-fangled scheme. It was proposed and strongly urged by the Commissioners who took evidence and reported on the state of our endowed schools in 1867 . . . one of its chief features was the recommendation of Provincial Authorities composed of representative persons appointed to carry out a great scheme of secondary education based on similar plans of academical districts in France, Prussia, and Switzerland. [46]

Other persons had proposed a similar body in the years between 1875 and 1895, and the same idea was inherent in the establishment of the Central Welsh Board in 1896 [47]. It was further pressed by Lloyd George in the debate on Clause 17 of the Balfour Act of 1902 [48]. In 1903, Sir William Anson proposed a Welsh Education Council, and in 1904—5 the Board of Education actually prepared a model scheme for a Welsh Joint Education Committee or Federation for the purpose of administering such matters as the training of teachers and the examination and inspection of schools of all kinds [49]. When the Liberals came to power in 1906 with Lloyd George in the Cabinet as President of the Board of Trade, Augustine Birrell's Education Bill included in Section 4 a Council of Education for Wales, but when the Bill was withdrawn on 20 December 1906 [50], the Welsh Department of the Board of Education was set up in January 1907. Further conferences were held in Wales right up to, and after the Bruce Report of 1920, and this Report advocated a National Council which came to nought [51].

To return to the Act of 1889 and its working mechanism. Thereafter both intermediate and technical education for Wales were administered by a local authority (for each county and county borough) called the Joint Education Committee of the County Council. The Charity Commissioners had the right to be represented at any meetings of such committees by an Assistant Commissioner and it was the duty of the committee to submit to the Charity Commissioners a scheme or schemes for intermediate and technical education in their localities. The Charity Commissioners in turn submitted the schemes to the Education Department and they were then laid before Parliament and approved by the Queen in Council. The Charity Commissioners were required to present an annual report to both Houses on proceedings under the Act, which was to be construed as one with the Endowed Schools Acts of 1869, 1873 and 1874, and cited with these as the Endowed Schools Acts 1869—89. In this guise the Welsh Intermediate Education Act came into operation on 1 November 1889 [52].

Within six months all the sixteen Joint Education Committees in

Wales were at work and between 1890 and 1892 ten conferences of these Committees were held, three for north Wales, the remainder covering the whole of Wales, under the chairmanship, first of A. H. D. Acland, MP (also Chairman of the Caernarvonshire Joint Education Committee) and then A. Humphreys Owen [53]. The representative of the Charity Commissioners at all these meetings was W. N. Bruce, son of Lord Aberdare, who was later to play a leading role in many aspects of Welsh education [54]. The first county scheme to be established was that of Caernarvonshire in 1893, the last that of Glamorgan in 1896. With the approval of schemes, the real executive work began. Schools had to be located, sites negotiated, buildings provided (though many schools first opened in chapel vestries or improvised school-rooms), and teachers had to be recruited – though before 1900 it was difficult to secure well-qualified graduate staff. Yet, in the short space of seven years, 88 new schools were opened in addition to the establishment of over sixty new local government bodies and sixteen county governing bodies each operating a county scheme [55]. By 1903 there were 95 intermediate schools with a total of 8,789 pupils, and by 1910 this number had expanded to 13,729 [56]. To co-ordinate this new system of intermediate education the Central Welsh Board was established in 1896 and was made responsible for the inspection and examination of all intermediate schools. Mr Owen Owen, Headmaster of Oswestry High School, became the first Chief Inspector of the Board – to the bitter disappointment of Owen M. Edwards, who was to become some ten years later the first Chief Inspector of the Welsh Department of the Board of Education [57]. The Central Welsh Board came into being three years before the Board of Education Act of 1899, and many more years before the Welsh Department. There was no question at that time of any overlapping of work. There was, however, 'an internal cleavage of opinion at the Joint Education Committees' Conferences as to whether it was necessary to bring into being a new national body to do this work at the very time when the new University of Wales was beginning to function' [58]. The issue was whether the University, which had received its charter three years before, might not itself perform the duties assigned to the Central Welsh Board. Ultimately, a compromise was reached: the Central Welsh Board was to be established, but after seven years there should be a conference between it and the University Court to consider the advisability of a transfer of the Board's functions. Nothing has been heard of the pact since that day [59].

The primary object of the plan to establish a Central Welsh Board, adopted and forwarded to the Charity Commissioners by all the Joint Education Committees, was to set up a Welsh body capable of undertaking the supervision required by the Treasury. This would avert the risk, incidental to the acceptance of state aid, that a rigid educational code might be imposed on the new schools by an authority unfamiliar with the peculiar local circumstances. There had been initial difficulties in 1891, when Sir John Goschen, then Chancellor of the Exchequer, felt that the proposal implied a large surrender of responsibility by the Treasury to a Welsh body naturally interested in the success of the schools. Eventually, the regulations under which the Treasury grant was awarded were issued in 1892 although four years were to elapse before they were approved. The difficulty indicated by Goschen was met by interposing the Charity Commissioners between the Treasury and the Central Welsh Board. In this way Wales obtained the freedom to guide its own educational development, while the Treasury obtained, through the department charged with the administration of the Intermediate Education Act, a guarantee that the conditions of state aid imposed by Parliament were fulfilled [60].

Finally, 'the Welsh Intermediate Education Act afforded another valuable precedent for separate legislation for Wales including Monmouthshire. Educationally, socially, and administratively it was one of the most impressive memorials of the political awakening of Wales.' [61] In 1898, D. R. Fearon, Secretary to the Charity Commissioners, speaking at the Keighley Institute, Yorkshire, of developments in Welsh intermediate and technical education, ventured to suggest 'that no educational reform more remarkable than this has ever been accomplished in any European country.' [62] What England had failed to accomplish in the 1860s — as Norman Morris has pointed out — and was not to achieve until 1902, Wales accomplished, with the aid of English reformers, in the 1890s. There were, of course, no powerful independent schools in Wales to organize opposition to the development of a national system of secondary education and which, in effect, postponed its establishment in England for forty years [63]. When the time arrived to establish a secondary system in England it was guided by men who had gained experience in Wales. A. H. D. Acland organized secondary education in the West Riding precisely as he had done earlier in Caernarvonshire. Others, like W. N. Bruce, Robert L. Morant, and particularly J. W. Headlam, A. G. Legard, and Thomas Darlington — the latter three being Senior Inspectors of the Board of Education — knew Wales and the Welsh secondary system thoroughly.

During the 1890s there was also considerable development in technical education on lines similar to England which greatly extended opportunities for technical training at the same time as intermediate schools were being established. Viriamu Jones at his University College in Cardiff saw that this could be a centre for developments in technical education and he was anxious that all sections of manual workers should understand the importance of technical training. He realized that by co-operating with the College, the industrialized counties in its vicinity would be able to provide efficient teaching on a comprehensive scale. In 1889, the Cardiff Technical Instruction Committee was formed and Glamorgan and Monmouthshire County Councils formed similar committees. Viriamu Jones planned Mining and Metallurgical Departments for his College where seven or eight hundred evening students attended. Large numbers of night schools for young colliers also flourished in Glamorgan and Monmouthshire. By 1892, technical classes had been established throughout south Wales. Quarrymen in north Wales were known to tramp sixteen miles after a day's work to learn mathematics, and colliers in south Wales, many 60 years of age, trudged to lectures on geology and mining. In February 1895, the Cardiff Technical School was providing fifty different courses in science and art, and had 2,600 students whose work was annually examined by government examiners [64].

No account of the development of Welsh education can evade the problem of the Welsh language and its survival. Paradoxically, with the development of Welsh elementary and secondary education, the Welsh language became neglected and was in danger of elimination. In the latter half of the nineteenth century most Welsh people were convinced that the only way to get on in the world was to learn English at the expense of the vernacular. We must again salute one of the wisest educationists of the nineteenth century, Kay-Shuttleworth. He foresaw the problem in 1849 when he instructed an Inspector, the Rev. H. Longueville Jones, to carry out a bilingual policy in the schools and training colleges of Wales. It is perhaps idle to speculate what the consequences to the education and language of Wales would have been, had Kay-Shuttleworth's policy been pursued over the years [65]. It was extremely unfortunate for Wales that he resigned his post nine months later on grounds of ill-health. Again, it is remarkable that the leading Welshmen who agitated for a Welsh university were prepared to advocate the natural right of the Welsh language to a place in Welsh education, and yet to advance the view that a better system of education might hasten its disappearance as a necessary preliminary to the due progress of the people [66]. As late as 1888 the Cross Commission threw out the first lifeline and recognized Welsh as a grant-earning subject under the elementary code on an equal footing with other languages [67]. The Central Welsh Board and the Welsh intermediate schools paid scant attention to the teaching of Welsh until the turn of the century. Welsh parents wanted their children to learn French, and this subject became so popular in the schools that for the first ten years of its existence the Central Welsh Board was often dubbed the Central French Board. This position the new officials of the Welsh Department were determined to amend after 1907 as we shall see later.

The third and final recommendation of the Aberdare Report, and the crown of the Welsh system of secondary and higher education brought into being after 1881 was a degree-awarding University of Wales. In the movement to this end, the familiar names are again prominent — Viriamu Jones, Lord Aberdare, Lord Rendel, A. H. D. Acland, and Sir H. Isambard Owen. The latter, a distinguished physician practising in London, who later left his mark on more than one English university, was responsible for drafting the charter of the University of Wales [68]. This movement was short and sweet, but not without its problems, for there were rival opinions regarding the type of university most desirable. Many meetings were inevitable but the crucial one held in Shrewsbury in 1891 decided two important issues: (a) it was to be a teaching rather than an examining university, conferring degrees on its own students with residential qualifications, and (b) the federal principle was adopted and the three University Colleges became constituent colleges of the University of Wales. The Royal Charter of the new University was granted on 20 November 1893.

II

The brief quinquennium from 1902 to 1907 in the evolution of Welsh educational structure and administration was in many ways both contentious and significant and the fat files relating to Welsh educational matters in the Public Record Office multiply so rapidly after 1902 — mainly centred around the efforts of one dominating personality — that these years may be aptly described as the 'Lloyd Georgian' phase of Welsh education. During this period, secondary education was not the main concern in Wales. The two burning issues were religious controversy leading to the 'Welsh Revolt' and a renewed demand for autonomy in the form of a National Council for Education. Neither issue was fought to a successful conclusion, but there was a good measure of administrative compensation in the establishment of the Welsh Department of the Board of Education in 1907.

The religious issue had, of course, been actual since the Act of 1870, if not before. Wales was mainly nonconformist and there had been bickerings and animosities between national and British schools before the establishment of the dual system of Church and Board schools. When the Forster Act was under discussion, Welsh nonconformist leaders made their position clear at a meeting held in Aberystwyth in January 1870. Their decision was for permissive biblical instruction and denominational teaching outside school hours — a view put to Gladstone and Forster by a deputation in March, and which found a reflection in the 'Cowper-Temple' clause ultimately adopted [69]. After 1870, Wales proved a fertile ground for the establishment of school boards — by 1897 there were 326 Welsh school boards, and by 1902, 379. During these years the dominance of voluntary schools melted away, and 'churchmen noted with alarm the growing tendency of Welsh school boards to favour an entirely secular system of instruction' [70]. It would be too long a narrative to unravel the religious disputations between Lloyd George, the Welsh Bishops, and the government. But from the Welsh point of view the religious issue and the desire for national autonomy were closely interlinked.

In prosecuting the Welsh cause in the Commons during debates on Balfour's Bill, Lloyd George worked out a clever strategy and perhaps his greatest memorial was his failure. On one occasion he secured a significant amendment — moved at his instigation by the chairman of the Welsh Parliamentary Party, Sir Alfred Thomas — transferring the powers of Welsh local authorities under the 1889 Act to the new local education authorities constituted by Balfour's Bill [71]. The point was that Section 17, Clause 5, of the Bill provided for the setting up of a Joint Education Committee covering a combination of counties and boroughs, and Lloyd George saw here an opportunity to create a National Council for Wales. This was also a way of drawing county councils into opposition to the religious provisions, and Lloyd George emphasized that they should operate the measures envisaged only on certain important conditions — that voluntary schools were to be brought under public control, religious tests for pupil-teachers abolished, and the 'colonial compromise' offered in relation to denominational instruction [72]. If these conditions were not complied with, nonconformists were to refuse to pay rates. Lloyd George's motto was 'No control, no cash' and this was the genesis of what came to be known as the 'Welsh Revolt' [73]. This amendment has never been placed in its proper context by those historians who have discussed the refusal of Welsh local education authorities to operate the provisions of the 1902 Act relating to voluntary schools and have merely referred to the Confidential Memorandum on the Defaulting Authorities, dated 25 June 1904, in the files of the Board of Education. The whole story is a long one which cannot be told here, but Anson was then compelled to push through Parliament the Local Authorities Default Bill, empowering the Board to administer the Act of 1902 when a local authority failed to comply. This became known as the 'Coercion of Wales Bill' and was operated more than once. After several years of continued opposition the smouldering embers of past animosities died down and the Balfour Act was more or less accepted.

There was a more hopeful development in the question of a National Council when, in 1903, Anson proposed a Joint Board of Welsh County Councils for educational purposes. Between 1903 and 1905 a succession of conferences and meetings, with Evan R. Davies cf Caernarvonshire as secretary, sought some agreement among Welsh L.E.A.s as to the powers of such a council and how it could function within the parliamentary system of the United Kingdom. Model schemes were actually drawn up by the Board of Education, but with the fall of the Conservative government at the close of 1905, these plans lapsed. In the new Liberal administration, Lloyd George, as President of the Board of Trade, was in the Cabinet and there was a direct approach to the question. Augustine Birrell's Education Bill provided in Part 4 for a National Council for Wales [74]. The Bill, heavily amended, was withdrawn by Campbell-Bannerman on 20 December 1906, and Lloyd George, in despair, sought an Order in Council to establish the Welsh National Council, but without success [75].

Meanwhile, the first mention of a Welsh Department of the Board of Education occurred on 12 December 1906, when, in the closing stages of the debate on Birrell's Bill in the House of Commons, Llewellyn Williams, MP for Carmarthen, stated in his speech that

> he hoped that if the Rt. Hon. Gentleman found it impossible to secure the passing of this Bill with Part 4 in it (i.e. the National Council for Wales) at all events he would see that the principle . . . should be carried out by an administrative Act which would not require the sanction of the House of Lords. If the government said it was impossible to get Part 4 through this House and the other House, they could, at all events assist Wales by establishing a subordinate branch of the Board of Education in Wales with permanent officials to deal with Welsh education. If that were done he did not much care what became of Part 4. All he was anxious to see was that the separate and distinct case of Wales should be recognized [76].

But this suggestion was never pursued, for a week later, on 19 December, Sir Alfred Thomas, MP for Glamorgan East, said 'that there should have been set up in Wales a Council for Education . . . but he understood that the Minister of Education was about to reorganize the Office and to set up a Welsh Department in the Board of Education . . . and he and his friends recognized that what was now proposed was a great advance towards securing autonomy in educational matters in Wales' [77].

III

The establishment of the Welsh Department at the beginning of January 1907, was one of Birrell's last acts before leaving for another post in Ireland. The Permanent Secretary of the Board, R. L. Morant, lost no time in giving effect to the decision of the Cabinet in a strictly Confidential Memorandum on Office Administration which stated that the degree of separation had not yet been precisely determined, and that

> as from February 4th, Mr Kingsford will act as Assistant Secretary for the Welsh Department . . . taking charge of all the work of the Board in respect of Wales with the exception of, for the present, Training Colleges, Training schools for Domestic Subjects, Teachers' pensions, the work at present done at South Kensington, and such other matters as may be named hereafter. It is probable that other officials, probably Welshmen, will shortly be appointed to this Branch. [78]

Two Welshmen were appointed to the two senior positions in the new Department. Alfred T. Davies, a Liverpool solicitor, became Permanent Secretary, and Owen M. Edwards, of Lincoln College, Oxford, was appointed Chief Inspector (after many other names had been submitted — some of whom withdrew — including Sir Henry Jones, D. Lleufer Thomas, and Dr Thomas Jones). Both officials had direct access to the President and were not subordinate to the Permanent Secretary, R. L. Morant [79]. If one reads between the lines of the minutes of the Board for these few weeks, the impression is given that Morant was not at all pleased with the new set-up, nor with the new officials who were not bound to consult him [80].

In its initial stages the new Department took charge of elementary and secondary education, and later, with the completion of new buildings in Whitehall, it became responsible for technical education, schools of art and further education, and training colleges [81]. The creation of the Welsh Department inevitably involved a certain measure of administrative dichotomy. On the one hand it functioned as an integral part of the whole Board of Education which meant that the resources of the Board in administrative ability and in specialized expertise were placed at the disposal of the new Department, whether in its administrative or inspectorial aspects, and also of the local education authorities. On the other hand it meant that the new Permanent Secretary and Chief Inspector had to initiate developments *de novo* in the administrative pattern of the Welsh side.

Relations with local education authorities and other bodies in Wales were as far as possible conducted through the Welsh Department, and there was a separately organized Welsh Inspectorate: 'the soundness of this conception is shown by its survival, unchanged in structure, and justified in practice over a period of sixty years' [82]. Owen Edwards built up carefully over a period of years a body of Welsh-speaking inspectors [83], and in 1909 had submitted to the President of the Board a survey of the work of his own post and the work being done in Wales [84]. The broad picture of the years 1907 to 1921 is one of evolution rather than revolution, but more than one event demands attention including a minor rebellion from the side of the Central Welsh Board. Having reorganized the inspectorate, other matters requiring attention were: the Welsh language, reform of the curricula of schools and training colleges, and the extension of technical and further education.

From the outset, Owen Edwards paid particular attention to the Welsh language in the schools of Wales. In the first Report of the Welsh Department in 1908 it was stated that

> the outstanding feature of the year in connection with the work of the Board in Wales has been the definite recognition of the Welsh language and literature in the curricula of elementary and secondary schools, and Training Colleges of the Principality . . . In the Code for 1907, as also in the Regulations for secondary schools and for Training Colleges in Wales for that year, the teaching of Welsh was fully and definitely recognized. [85]

In 1909, Edwards was able to report that 'the introduction of Welsh to elementary schools, secondary schools, and Training Colleges has already begun to react on, and give new vigour to the three great educational institutions that stand outside the Board's purview, i.e. the Sunday school, the Literary Meetings, and the Eisteddfod' [86]. He also added that in administering the Code, it had some special aims, such as, e.g. to deal wisely and efficiently with the distinct problem of Welsh education – the bilingual problem. It has changed a 'bilingual difficulty' into a bilingual opportunity. In most elementary schools children get the educational advantage that comes from a knowledge of two languages. The utilization of Welsh dates much further back than the establishing of the Welsh Department; but it was the Department that made universal – where L.E.A.s desire it – an efficient and logical system of bilingual teaching, varying according to whether the district is Welsh-speaking, bilingual, or English-speaking. The problem is important to other parts of the Empire, and the experience of the Welsh Department has been of much value to such parts as Mauritius and Cape Colony. [87]

Edwards also emphasized the importance in the same Code, of relating the education of the Welsh child to his own environment and traditions and way of life – rather than to an English background.

In the field of elementary education the old bitterness over the voluntary schools engendered by the settlement in the 1902 Act was slowly diminishing. Here, the Welsh Department was able to encourage the erection of new council schools in many districts hitherto served only by the Church of England, so remedying a long-standing grievance. But this could not always be done, disputes between school managers and L.E.A.s continued, and the Department's decisions in accordance with the law and current policy were not always accepted with equally good grace by both sides [88].

It was in the secondary field that the problem of relations with the Central Welsh Board arose. From the beginning this Board was a sharp thorn in the flesh of the Welsh Department, both for historical reasons and also because the Welsh Department was critical of the Board's multiplicity and rigidity of examinations, and the uniform nature of the Welsh intermediate schools. Edwards was also deeply conscious of the fact that the Welsh intermediate schools had been modelled on the older English grammar schools and that Welsh had been neglected in their time-tables. Matters were further complicated when after the 1902 Act, the Board of Education not only made grants to the Central Welsh Board but also shared the inspection of the intermediate schools. This meant that after 1907, the Welsh Department of the Board took over informal inspection of these schools as well as the inspection of the new secondary schools, established after the Act of 1902.

It may be recalled here that Owen Edwards had been an unsuccessful candidate for the post of Chief Inspector to the Central Welsh Board some ten years earlier. That his attitude to that Board was unsympathetic and suspicious appears undeniable from the content of internal correspondence and minutes in the files of the Board from 1908 onwards [89]. The flashpoint came in 1909 when the Central Welsh Board rebelled against the Welsh Department's annual report which was sharply critical of its work, urging that 'the Central Welsh Board should now consider to what extent their rigid examination system might be the cause of the wooden and unintelligent type of mind of which their examiners complained. Elasticity and adaptability of curricula, and the development of differentiation among schools were difficult under such a highly centralized system of examinations.' [90] The most furious attack on the Welsh Department came from Edgar Jones, Headmaster of Barry Boys' County School, in his Presidential Address to the Welsh County Schools Association at Shrewsbury, in October 1910 [91]. Just over a week later, on 6 November, Owen Edwards sent a letter to Henry G. Maurice (Private Secretary to Morant) stating 'I got the Headmaster's Address at Shrewsbury yesterday. I have begun to answer it, as you request, point by point. It is outrageous and mischievous, and it must be pulverized.' [92]

The controversy rang out through the Principality. Owen Edwards wrote a lengthy detailed reply to Edgar Jones and the majority of MPs and leading Welshmen, including local authorities, supported the Welsh Department [93]. Several years later, after the tumult died down, a compromise was reached regarding schools inspection, but the Welsh Department refused to withdraw from the position of advising the Central Welsh Board on its function of approving curricula and timetables in the intermediate schools.

In the field of higher education a new step was taken during the war when a Royal Commission on the University of Wales, presided over by Lord Haldane from 1916 to 1918 [94], recommended an overhaul of the administration of the university, the establishment of an Academic Board, and the founding of another University College which was opened in Swansea in 1921. The reconstituted University of Wales, still organized on the federal principle, now involved four constituent Colleges.

The reconstitution of the University, and the passage of the Education Act of 1918, necessitated a fresh inquiry into the organization of secondary education in Wales. In 1918, a Departmental Committee was appointed by the President of the Board, under the chairmanship of the Hon. W. N. Bruce, to advise on how the organization of secondary education in Wales 'may be consolidated and co-ordinated with other branches of education, *with a view to the*

establishment of a national system of public education in Wales' [95].
When the Report appeared in September 1920, one of its main
recommendations was a National Council for Education in Wales,
whose functions would be primarily advisory and deliberative, replacing
the Central Welsh Board and the University Court. It should have 120
representatives and the Council was to be free to discuss all types of
education and would submit its views to the Board of Education. But
by this time the Board of Education and the University had adopted a
negative attitude, the former preferring to continue its influence and
guidance from Whitehall, and the latter determined to identify itself
with purely academic rather than national responsibilities [96]. Moreover, the L.E.A.s were becoming more important, were growing in
stature and influence, and could exercise considerable power in
educational councils especially through the Federation of Welsh Education Authorities. Here might have been the germ of a really constructive
National Council — a Council which would have united the Welsh
L.E.A.s into one single L.E.A. for Wales, giving it a national character.
The National Council for Education never materialized though it was
again mooted more than once after 1921.

Notes

[1] H. R. Reichel, *Patriotism — True and False, the Welsh Outlook,*
pp.104–6, Newtown, 1921.

[2] K. O. Morgan, *Wales in British Politics, 1868–1922*, p.3, University of Wales Press, 1963.

[3] The College at Caernarvon was moved to Bangor in 1894 and
named St Mary's.

[4] *Welsh in Education and Life*, Report of the Departmental
Committee, Board of Education, p. 62, 1927.

[5] L. Wynne Evans, 'Voluntary Education in the industrial areas of
Wales before 1870', *National Library of Wales Journal*, Vol.XIV,
No.4, 1966 and 'School Boards and the Works Schools System
after the Education Act of 1870', *N.L.W.J.* Vol.XV, No.1, 1967.

[6] D. Emrys Evans, *The University of Wales*, p.15, University of
Wales Press, Cardiff, 1953.

[7] K. O. Morgan, op. cit., p.28

[8] Ibid., p. 46.

[9] Report of the Committee appointed to Inquire into the Condi-
tion of Intermediate and Higher Education in Wales and
Monmouthshire, 1881 (Aberdare Report), Vol.II, evidence of
Hugh Owen, pp.12–15.

Also: *Parliamentary Debates*, 4th Vol. Session 1889, p.126; also pp.153—4.

[10] K. Viriamu Jones, *Life of J. Viriamu Jones*, p.99, London, 1921

[11] K. O. Morgan, op. cit., p.47

[12] *Parl. Debates*, ibid., 1889, p.122, Stuart Rendel moving the second reading of the Intermediate Education (Wales) Bill, 15 May.

[13] *The Calendar*, University of Wales, 1968—69, p.431.

[14] Report of the Association of Welsh Clergy in the West Riding, 1854, p.5. An association of Welsh clergy had been formed in the West Riding in 1821 which comprised disgruntled clerics who had left Wales because they could no longer tolerate a system which promoted strangers to all the lucrative livings in preference to native clergy, and many of them were men of outstanding academic ability.

[15] Ibid.

[16] D. Emrys Evans, op. cit., p.12

[17] D. Lewis Lloyd, *The Missing Link in Education in Wales*, Nixon & Jarvis, Bangor, 1876

[18] Ibid., p.5 ff.

[19] *Parl. Debates*, 3rd series, Vol.cclxvii, p.1141 ff.

[20] K. O. Morgan, op. cit., p.48

[21] P.R.O. Ed 91/8, No.1 of Five Files: Preliminaries to the Aberdare Report, 1880

[22] Aberdare Report, ibid., p.xxiv.

[23] Ibid., pp.xlvi-vii

[24] Ibid., p.xvi. Also, *Parl.Deb.*, 4th Vol. of Session 1889, p.130.

[25] *Parl. Deb.*, ibid., pp.105—6. Sir Hussey Vivian (Swansea District) was himself a churchman.

[26] Aberdare Report, ibid., p.xvi; Also, *Parl. Deb.*,ibid., p.124.

[27] Aberdare Report, ibid., p.lxvi.

[28] Ibid., p.lxviii.

[29] Ibid., p.lxix.

[30] K. Viriamu Jones, op. cit., p.103

[31] D. Emrys Evans, op. cit., p.33

[32] K. Viriamu Jones, op. cit., p.50

[33] D. Emrys Evans, cf. ref. 31 above

[34] K. O. Morgan, op. cit., p.50

[35] Ibid.

[36] Ibid., p.52

[37] Report of the Departmental Committee on the Organization of Secondary Education in Wales (The Bruce Report), 1920, p.17. Also: W. N. Bruce, *The Welsh Intermediate Education Act, 1889, Its origin and working*, p.13.

[38] David Williams, *Thomas Francis Roberts*, pp.13–19, Cardiff, 1961.
Also: D. Emrys Evans, ibid., p.24.
[39] K. Viriamu Jones, op. cit., pp.202–3
[40] Ibid.
[41] *Parl. Deb.*, 3rd Series, Vol.cccxxxvi, p.121 ff.
[42] Ibid.
Also: T. Ellis and Ellis Griffith, *Intermediate and Technical Education (Wales),* the National Association for the Promotion of Technical and Secondary Education, 14, Dean's Yard, S.W., 1889.
[43] Ibid., p.13 ff.
[44] The Technical Instruction Act was passed on 30 August 1889.
[45] *Parl.Deb.*, ibid., 1889, p.147 ff.
[46] Ibid.
[47] K. Viriamu Jones, op. cit., p.211. As early as 1887 Mr Owen Owen had put forward a proposal for a Welsh Education Department at Whitehall. Also in 1875, Mr Humphreys Owen had proposed a Central Body for Wales. In 1895, a Central Board was discussed which became the Central Welsh Board, in spite of Viriamu Jones's objection on the grounds that the new University of Wales should be in control.
[48] Part 4, Section 17 (5), 2 Edw.7, c.42.
[49] P.R.O. Ed 91/10; Ed 91/11; Ed 24/579.
[50] *Parl. Deb.*, 4th Series, Vol.clxvii, 1906, p.450 ff.
[51] Bruce Report, ibid., p.86 ff.
[52] *The Welsh Intermediate Education Act, 1889: Its origin and working*, ibid., p.10 ff.
[53] Report of Proceedings, Joint Education Committees of Wales and Monmouthshire, 1890–2.
[54] R. L. Morant succeeded W. N. Bruce as the Board's representative at meetings of the Central Welsh Board and its Executive committee, prior to his appointment as the Permanent Secretary of the Board of Education in 1903: Sir Percy Watkins, *A Welshman Remembers: An Autobiography*, p.85, W. Lewis, Cardiff, 1944.
[55] Ibid., pp.56–57.
[56] J. V. Morgan, *A Study in Nationality*, p.387, London, 1911.
[57] Sir Percy Watkins, op. cit.: a full account of the appointment is given on p.38 ff.
[58] Ibid., p.54
[59] K. Viriamu Jones, op. cit., p.211 ff.
[60] *The Welsh Intermediate Education Act, 1889, Its origin and working*, ibid, p.28.

[61] K. O. Morgan, op. cit., p.102

[62] Sir Percy Watkins, op. cit., p.58

[63] see above, p. 23—4

[64] K. Viriamu Jones, op. cit., p.152 ff.

[65] *Welsh in Education and Life*, ibid., p.60

[66] D. Emrys Evans, op. cit., p.15

[67] Third Report of the Commissioners of Inquiry into the elementary education Acts 1887 (c.5158), Vol.iii. Also, Final Report, ibid., 1888, (c.5485), pp.144—5.

[68] Isambard Owen's father was the chief architect of the Great Western Railway with the famous engineer Isambard Kingdom Brunel, who was Owen's godparent. In addition to his work in creating the Welsh University, he became Principal of Armstrong College, Newcastle upon Tyne from 1904—9, and was responsible for the reconstitution of the Durham Colleges culminating in the passing of the University of Durham Act in 1908. He left to become Vice-Chancellor of Bristol University in 1909 where he reorganized and re-drafted its Charter, and also took a leading part in the establishment of the National Library and National Museum of Wales.

[69] T. Gwynn Jones, *Cofiant Thomas Gee*, p.309, Denbigh, 1913

[70] K. O. Morgan, op. cit., p.183

[71] Ibid., p.186

[72] In many of the colonies, undenominational instruction based on simple Bible teaching was reinforced by denominational right of entry one or more days per week.

[73] K. O. Morgan, op. cit., pp.187—8

[74] P.R.O. Ed 24/118: Draft Schedule circulated by request of Lloyd George.

[75] *Parl. Deb.*, 4th Series, Vols.clxi; clxii; clxv, 1906.

[76] Ibid., Vol.clvii, pp.449—51.

[77] Ibid., Vol.ccxvii, 1906, p.1755.

[78] P.R.O.Ed 23/216 F, No.3, pp.6—7, Confidential Memorandum, Board of Education, R. L. Morant, January, 1907.

[79] P.R.O. Ed 23/242; Ed 24/580. Probably Dr Thomas Jones was not considered for one of the two new posts in the new Welsh Department, although Lloyd George in a letter to Morant dated 25 January 1907 commends this 'fresh name'. When Lloyd George became Prime Minister in 1916, Dr Jones was appointed to the Cabinet Secretariat.

[80] P.R.O. Ed 24/581.

[81] P.R.O. Ed 24/580.

[82] Ministry of Education, *Education 1900—1950*, p.115, H.M.S.O., 1951.

[83] P.R.O. Ed 23/145; Ed 23/146; Ed 23/147; Ed 23/148;

[84] P.R.O. Ed 24/584.

[85] Report of the Board of Education, Cd.4566, 1907—8, p.13.

[86] P.R.O. Ed 24/584, p.7.

[87] Ibid., p.2.

[88] *Education, 1900—1950*, ibid., p.115 ff.

[89] P.R.O. Ed 24/589. One example is a letter written to Henry Maurice by Owen Edwards on 31 October 1910: 'Would you mind reminding the President that the Central Welsh Board people are on the war-path again. They are at their old trick — combining to write to the Welsh Members, to make a difficulty in Parliament. (I sincerely hope the Welsh Members will not be caught this time.) Last time they objected to our inspecting Welsh schools, this time they resent our report on the working of the Welsh Act. Please assure the President that, in case of a question, there is a complete and crushing answer.'

[90] Board of Education (Welsh Department), Report for 1909, p.19.

[91] Edgar Jones; *Reply to the Report on Intermediate Education issued by the Welsh Department of the Board of Education, 1909*. Cardiff, The Educational Publishing Company Limited.

[92] P.R.O. Ed 24/588.

[93] Ibid.

[94] Royal Commission on University Education in Wales, 1916; Final Report, Cd.8991, 1918, H.M.S.O.

[95] Bruce Report, ibid.

[96] 'The Welsh Department, Ministry of Education, 1907—1957', *Transactions of the Honourable Society of Cymmrodorion*, Session 1957, London, 1958, p.35.

JOHN STOCKS

Scotland's *ad hoc* authorities, 1919-1930*

One of the most interesting aspects of the history of Scottish education
is the constant interplay between the tendency towards assimilation
with the English system and the periodic reassertion of an independent
Scots tradition. In many respects educational policy after the setting-up
in 1839 of the committee of council followed the English pattern, even
after the formation of a separate committee for education in Scotland
in 1872 and the subsequent appointment to it of a separate secretary.
The Act of 1872, for example, which established parochial and burgh
school boards, clearly owed something to the English precedent of two
years earlier. But the abolition of the English school boards in 1902 was
an example that was not immediately followed by Scotland. The
Scottish boards lasted until the end of the First World War, and even
then there was a further departure from the English pattern of
administration. The same legislature as had entrusted education to the
county councils in England, decided to create for Scotland an entirely
new kind of authority. Like the school board, it was to be elected
solely for the purposes of education, and it was given the power to levy
a special education rate. Where it differed from the board system was
that the unit of administration instead of being the burgh or the parish,
became, except for the largest burghs, the county.

One other change had to be made. It was generally agreed that the
system of cumulative voting, by which each voter not only had as many
votes as there were candidates but could distribute them in any way he
liked, had not been successful. The possibility of 'plumping' for one
candidate with all the votes at one's disposal, had led to the undue
representation of minorities and the election of a number of 'faddists'.
There was another way to protect minorities without going to this
extreme. It was decided that there should be a full-scale experiment
with proportional representation.

* I am indebted to my friend Mr John M. Simpson of the Department of
Scottish History in the University of Edinburgh for his invaluable help and
encouragement in the preparation of this paper.

Though the *ad hoc* authorities were in operation from 1919 to 1930, most of what I have to say refers to the passing of the measure which created them, the Education (Scotland) Act of 1918. I have tried to look in some detail at the controversy which arose at that time concerning the local administration of education, an issue seriously debated by the public in a way that it has never been since. First, however, one must look back to the beginning of the century and the end of the school boards in England.

I

One possible explanation for the longer duration of the school board era in Scotland is that the Scottish boards constituted a system which covered the whole country, with a board for every parish and every burgh, as opposed to the situation in England where boards were created only in areas of educational deficiency. Thus Scotland in 1900 had a national system which could obviously be modified to suit the needs of the twentieth century more easily than could the English set-up. But before constructing theories to explain why the two countries diverged in this way at the beginning of the century, one must not forget the part that chance played in the events of 1902. Had the horse which was drawing Joseph Chamberlain's hansom-cab to the Athenaeum on 7 July not slipped and fallen, Chamberlain would no doubt have been in the House instead of the hospital, when section 5 of the Education Bill was being discussed in committee. If he had realized that the Government was about to jettison the 'local option' clause which alone had secured his reluctant support for the Bill, his enormous influence might have been used to gain for the school boards a stay of execution. A former member of Birmingham School Board, he was the most powerful man whom the boards could reasonably expect to defend them, and his temporary incapacity at this crucial time may well have speeded their abolition [1].

What makes a remarkable contrast with Scotland, however, is the lack of any real support for the *ad hoc* principle. Those in England who saw the need for larger units of administration than the parish, tended to see *ad omnia* authorities such as the county councils as the only alternative. There were few prominent supporters for the idea of retaining the *ad hoc* principle while creating new education authorities to control both elementary and secondary education.

Balfour, during the debate on the second reading of the Bill, dismissed such an idea as 'impracticable', saying that he knew of only two members of parliament who favoured it. One was a Liberal, T. J. Macnamara, who was also a member of the London School Board, and a former president of the N.U.T. Macnamara interrupted Balfour, however, to say that he had been misunderstood. What he favoured was a combination of the existing system of boards for elementary education (the system presumably being extended to cover the whole country) plus joint committees of school boards and county councils for higher education. This was a similar solution to that which had already been adopted, or rather had 'growed', north of the border, though more likely Macnamara had in mind the rather similar recommendations of the Bryce Report of 1895.

Macnamara's complaint of being misrepresented is odd, in view of the fact that he wished to father the views which Balfour was attacking upon Balfour's own minister, Sir John Gorst. Gorst, he claimed, had advocated in a speech at Bradford (on 11 January 1899) the retention of the large school boards and the extension of their powers to cover the whole of education. But if the report of Gorst's speech given in *The Times* of the following day is to be trusted, Gorst said no such thing. What he said was that there was 'much to be said for' making the 'education authority for all purposes such school boards as now exist in many large cities' but he went on to speak of what he called 'obvious objections to this course'. Even the possibility of new *ad hoc* bodies he dismissed as introducing another set of authorities into 'an already confused system of local government'. Curiously enough, Gorst, who was in the chamber, or at least had been a few seconds earlier, did not contradict this statement of his position either at the time or at a later stage in the debate.

The other supporter of *ad hoc* authorities for all forms of school education, was referred to by the Prime Minister as the member 'on this side' for Newcastle, who had not spoken in that debate — a reference which was most inconsiderate to posterity, as there are two Newcastles, one of them returning two members, and all three MPs were on the government side. It seems that the Conservative member for Newcastle-on-Tyne, W. R. Plummer, was meant, but he made no reference to *ad hoc* authorities during the discussion of the Bill, except to express his regret at the passing of the boards.

Even if there had been a strong, coherent body of opinion in support of an *ad hoc* system of administration over fairly large areas, it would have been faced with the determined opposition of Sir Robert Morant of the Board of Education. In a memorandum of 1899 or 1900 he made clear his view that there should be no continuance of the *ad hoc* principle. The reasons he gave were (1) that there were already municipal authorities for higher education and that any plan for the *ad hoc* control of elementary education would therefore mean two separate education authorities in large cities; (2) that *ad hoc* administration made educational expenditure exceptional and extravagant in the eyes of the rate-payers, and (3) that *ad hoc* education authorities tended to be monopolized by faddists [2]. Morant's authority, even before he became Secretary to the Board of Education, was such that these objections could not lightly have been brushed aside.

The passage of the Education Bill of 1902 did not go unnoticed in Scotland. Indeed it is hard to imagine any comparable educational measure for England and Wales today attracting as much attention north of the border as did the Balfour Act. This was partly, no doubt, because of the instinctive sympathy Scots felt for the English nonconformists. Like their ancestors who led an army into England to fight in the Civil War on the side of the Roundheads, the Scots sharpened their pens and plunged into the fray on the side of dissent. The columns of *The Educational News*, in particular, rang with denunciations of this 'clerical device for subsidizing the Church at the expense of the public' which was 'contrary to all ideas of justice and commonsense' and reflected 'the blighting influence of aggressive sectarianism' [3]. Hardly a week passed while the Bill was before parliament – and its passage was a long one – without some reference to it in this journal.

If the involvement of Scottish sympathies is part of the explanation for this remarkable degree of spectator participation, there is another reason, and that is that the spectators expected soon to be involved themselves. True, the denominational problem which caused most of the conflict in England and Wales had no exact parallel in Scotland, but the administrative change-over from school boards to county councils was also a subject of interest. Thus, on 19 July, *The Educational News* remarked that it was 'all but certain that the next Scotch Education Bill will bear to a considerable extent the impress of its English predecessor', and, with growing confidence, declared on 23 August that 'the English Bill, so soon as passed, will be applied to Scotland'.

By November it seemed clear to *The Educational News* from a speech given in Greenock by Lord Balfour, the Secretary for Scotland, that it was 'evident' there was 'a Scotch Bill already prepared and awaiting an opportunity of Parliamentary discussion'. Lord Balfour, it was said, 'hoped for early action'.

Lord Balfour did indeed express the hope for early action to simplify and modernize Scotland's creaking educational machinery, pleading for co-operation in a comprehensive educational measure and for a non-partisan approach that would be in contrast to the sectional differences on education seen in England and Wales. There is, however, no mention, in a very full account of his speech in the columns of *The Scotsman*, of any Bill 'already prepared' — only a general intention to legislate [4]. Indeed the files of the Scotch Education Department show clearly that Lord Balfour could not honestly have said more. The first draft of a Bill was not produced by the Department till the following summer [5]. *The Educational News* had taken the will for the deed.

The need for reform was clear, and fully appreciated by Scots educationists. The school boards, unlike their English counterparts, had control over secondary as well as elementary education. Since 1892, however, there had also been involved in this field the county and burgh secondary education committees. These committees, formed of representatives of the town or county council and of the school boards in the area, were mainly grant-awarding bodies which exercised little control. The town and county councils themselves, too, had a finger in the pie by their disbursing of the 'whisky money' for technical education. Such were the complications produced by the unsatisfactory treatment of post-primary education by the Act of 1872. But in addition there was a whole range of problems caused by the fact that, in spite of a few amalgamations, there were still over 970 boards, many of which controlled only a handful of schools.

In eager anticipation of reform, the Scots fell hungrily on such scraps of information about the impending legislation as could be gleaned from government spokesmen. Lord Balfour, some thought, had made it clear in his Greenock speech of November 1902 that a comprehensive Bill to enlarge the administrative area was ready to be debated by Parliament. But did the government intend to continue or to abolish the principle of an *ad hoc* local authority? The Educational Institute of Scotland (E.I.S.), the main organization of teachers, professed to see hints of the continuance of *ad hoc*, but this was just the kind of organization the Institute wanted. Although the need for larger areas had been appreciated for some years, education, it was claimed, was 'of sufficient importance to demand the whole and undivided attention of a local authority specially appointed for its control' [6].

At the same time, there was in some quarters the almost fatalistic belief that what had happened in England would, in the legislators' good time, be applied as the cure for Scotland's ills as well. This would suggest a different policy [7].

The Lord Advocate, the government's adviser on Scottish legal affairs, speaking in January 1903, assured the country that, because of the differing conditions, a Scottish Education Bill would not be framed in the same way as the English Act. What the Government had in mind was a measure which would be 'thoroughly Scotch in its character' [8]. But what did that mean? Later the same month Lord Balfour spoke again, this time in Glasgow, expressing himself in favour of a system which had its 'basis on direct popular election'. Was this a clear commitment to *ad hoc*? *The Educational News* at first thought not, considering perhaps that, as a county council was directly elected, this could be regarded as the 'basis' on which an education committee would be the superstructure [9]. The following week the leader writer had changed his mind, being apparently less ready to subject the straightforward expression 'a basis [of] direct popular election' to such a tortuous interpretation. The Government surely intended *ad hoc* to stay.

The attraction of this kind of authority to the E.I.S., whose views were represented by *The Educational News*, was not due to any love of the school boards. The boards, particularly the smaller ones, had not endeared themselves to the profession. The penny-pinching, the sectarian rivalries, the occasional dismissal, invariably regarded by the E.I.S. as totally unjustified [10], and the close watch kept in some areas on the smallest details of the management of the schools – all these made the teachers keen on reform. After such a regime, it was said, 'a little wholesome neglect would be a welcome relief'.

The Bill of 1904, introduced by Lord Dunedin, provided for the continuance of *ad hoc*, though it went some way towards satisfying the demands for a reduction in the number of authorities. The unit of administration was, apart from five large burghs, to be the district of the county. The bill was given an unopposed second reading but foundered at the committee stage for lack of time. The government, said the Liberals, were 'too keen on compensating English publicans and coercing Welsh defaulters to afford even a week of Parliamentary time to carry a Scotch bill of no particular sectional interest' [11]. The following session the Bill was re-introduced but again failed to become law before the election of 1905 returned a Liberal government.

After the fruitless attempts in 1906 and 1907 to undo the work of the 1902 Act, the government was more successful with educational legislation for Scotland. This was achieved, however, at the expense of avoiding controversy. An Act was finally passed in 1908, but it was an Act which practically side-stepped the administrative problem and concentrated instead on widening the legal aspect of education to cover the physical well-being of the child [12]. The boards were given powers to provide meals, clothing, bursaries, hostels and travel allowances, etc. On the financial side, the Act brought together all kinds of grant into the one Education (Scotland) Fund. Against this merciful simplification, however, the Act gave statutory recognition for the first time to the secondary education committees in the counties and the largest burghs, thereby hardening the unsatisfactory overlap of authority with the school boards.

II

Agitation for a reorganization of the system continued. The Secretary for Scotland in 1913 considered suggestions for reform put to him by the Scotch Education Department, but the war intervened before anything was done. Before the end of the war, however, important decisions were reached between Munro, the Secretary for Scotland in Lloyd George's government, and the head of the Department, Sir John Struthers, a key figure in the legislation that was to follow.

Struthers was one of the last examples of the 'lad o'pairts', the clever child from the country who goes straight from parish school to university, a phenomenon, whether common or not, generally held to be the glory of the Scottish tradition of parochial education. From the parish school of Mearns in Renfrewshire where he was a pupil-teacher, Struthers went to the Church of Scotland Training College in Glasgow, attending classes at the university concurrently. Not content with degrees from this university in Mental Philosophy and in Classics, he went to Oxford and read both Mods. and Greats. Thus equipped, but with little experience as a full-time teacher, he joined the inspectorate in 1886. Later he transferred to the Department, then under its first Secretary, Sir Henry Craik, and after fairly rapid promotion became Craik's successor in 1904.

In the seventeen years in which he held this post (1904–21) undoubtedly the main educational event was the passing of the Act of 1918. In this he played an all-important part. 'The policy of the Act was his' said Munro, the Secretary for Scotland, '. . . he did more to fashion and mould its provisions than any other man' [13].

Of his administrative ability there can be little doubt. His memoranda to his political chief were almost always models of lucidity. Lloyd George described him as 'one of the ablest officials in the Government service' [14]. In deference and self-effacement too, he was the perfect civil servant. On one occasion, when Munro had to deliver a speech on the Education Bill, Struthers suggested in outline what he should say, altered Munro's first draft almost beyond recognition, and corrected a second draft, before declaring that the speech was substantially the Minister's own composition [15].

Yet in spite, or perhaps because of this efficiency, combined with a natural reserve, Struthers was not popular. Undoubtedly one difficulty was caused by the situation of the Department in far-off London. This was a constant source of irritation to the Scots until 1939, when in an attempt to buy off one of the periodic demands for home rule, the government transferred the Scottish office from Whitehall to Edinburgh [16].

Not all Struthers' unpopularity can be explained in this way. His predecessor was better liked. Clues to his character appear between the lines of an appreciation written by his former political chief, Robert Munro. The popular figure of Struthers, we are told, was that of 'a bureaucrat seated in Whitehall, turning down the ideas and schemes submitted to him, and dictating educational policy with a supreme disregard of all representations made to him'. 'Ludicrously inaccurate' was Munro's verdict on this picture of Struthers, but he seems to have had some understanding of it. 'He may have had an iron hand', he went on, 'but it was often encased in a velvet glove' — 'often' encased, we note, but not always. Finally, when we are told in the context of an appreciation that 'under a certain brusqueness of manner . . . there was a heart of gold', we may be sure of the brusqueness of manner [13].

The preparation of the legislation which was to reorganize education in Scotland began in earnest in May 1917. Struthers saw three important questions to be decided: (i) what should be the area of administration? (ii) should it be an *ad hoc* or an *ad omnia* authority? (iii) if it was to be an *ad hoc* authority, how was it to be elected? [17]

On the first point, Struthers was quite decided. The minimum area was the county. He was too well aware of public opinion, however, not to anticipate opposition. Many, he foresaw, would favour only a grouping together of two or three school boards, while there were even 'a few stalwarts' who would cling to the school board in every parish. The nucleus of this opposition would be the boards and the clergy reinforced by the 'political', by which he meant left-wing, hostility to the county councils. His own views on the subject, however, were shared by an 'intelligent growing minority' among whom he included the teachers, newly converted to this position.

Likewise he was in no doubt about the administrative unsuitability of an *ad hoc* body. Unlike Morant, however, he was by no means lucid in his observations on this question. One argument, designed to show that, if the elections for such a body were combined with those for the county council, the resulting educational machinery would be 'ludicrously' unwieldy, is so obscure that, not surprisingly, in December of that same year Struthers noted in the margin that he 'would not now lay so much stress' on it. What is surprising, however, is that he allowed his minister to lift this section, as much else from this memorandum, for his speech in Edinburgh at the beginning of the following year. Munro, who presumably made his speech without seeing this marginal comment, must have left some furrowed brows behind him.

In addition, Struthers feared that *ad hoc* would perpetuate the predominance of the clergy which was a feature of the school boards. The first poll, indeed, had resulted in the election of no fewer than 1,450 clergymen – one quarter of all those elected [18]. This argument, too, Munro pressed into the draft of his Edinburgh speech, but when Struthers observed that this could hardly be said in public, the reference was duly withdrawn.

Lastly, it is worth noting from this memorandum that, as the parliamentary session was shortly due to end, Struthers emphasized to the Secretary for Scotland that this Bill could go no further than a first reading. As Fisher was to speak later of having flown a kite (*ballon d'essai*) with his Bill for England in the same year [19], so Munro was persuaded to give the Scottish Bill a trial run, with the county councils proposed as local authorities. This, predicted Struthers, would 'focus discussion'.

Struthers was right. The introduction of the Bill in December 1917 caused considerable controversy. There were two main issues. The first was the integration into the public educational system of the denominational schools. Unlike the schools run by the presbyterian churches, the Roman Catholic and the few Episcopalian schools had not been transferred to the control of the school boards. Though they continued to receive grants-in-aid, these denominational schools had for some time been languishing for want of adequate financial support, and this Bill which led to their being publicly provided and maintained, proved to be their salvation [20].

The other main issue was the proposed abolition of the school boards, which had been in existence for almost half a century. On this question letters and petitions poured into the Scotch Education

Department, some of them, incidentally, having been sent initially to Mr Fisher at the Board of Education, a remarkable tribute, it would appear, to Fisher's reputation or possibly a calculated snub to the Secretary for Scotland. Few holders of this office have enjoyed much popularity in Scotland, and Munro's allegiance to Lloyd George would make him, at least in some quarters, doubly suspect.

The great majority of these representations attacked the administrative proposals of the Bill. They came in the main from two sources, members of school boards, and left-wing organizations – trade unions, trades and labour councils, branches of the I.L.P., etc. School board opposition was to be expected, but the hostility of the Left deserves closer examination.

The main reason was no doubt the fear, expressed openly by the Kinross branch of the National Union of Railwaymen, that county council administration would deprive the working class of participation in the conduct of education. Whether this fear was justified is an interesting question. Struthers held that it was not [21]. In a memorandum to Munro he showed some of the weaknesses of the Labour position on this matter. Local government, he pointed out, was at that time largely run on the *ad hoc* principle, with school boards for education, parish councils for the Poor Law, district councils for public health and county councils responsible for roads, bridges and police. What, he asked, was the result for the working classes? On which of these bodies had they obtained a position in the least corresponding to their numbers and growing authority? As far as the school boards were concerned, out of a total of almost 950 boards, each with anything from five to fifteen members, there were only a mere handful – about eighty, thought Struthers – who represented the Labour cause. If this estimate of Labour representation was at all accurate, it makes the Left's support for the *ad hoc* principle in education rather surprising, though it could hardly be claimed that Labour's poor representation was a direct result of *ad hoc*. Possibly the isolation of different aspects of local government led to low polls, with people seeing few issues of any importance turning on their vote, and any tendency to abstain may have been proportionately stronger among the working class than the rest of the population. On the other hand, Labour's strength in Scotland was not so great numerically as their leaders' activity would suggest. As a result of the greater radicalism of the Liberal Party in Scotland than elsewhere in Britain, and of the split in the Scottish working class over the Irish question [22], the Labour Party continued to be weak until the general election of 1922.

Struthers also tackled Labour hostility to the county councils. This was a feeling similar to that expressed by some Socialist spokesmen in England in 1902, when county councils there were being made the local authorities for education, and arose from the same cause, namely the traditional land-owning 'image' of the county councillor. This was partly due, Struthers claimed, to historical circumstances, the county councils being the successors of the Commissioners of Supply, who were large land-owners. It was also partly to be accounted for by the fact that county councils so far had only a limited sphere of action, in matters which appealed more to the land-owning classes than to the population as a whole. In addition, there were the travelling expenses which county councillors met out of their own pockets and which were calculated to discourage working-class people from seeking election. This last problem, he implied, could easily be solved [23].

The conclusion which Struthers drew was that, if the *ad hoc* elections in which the public took little interest were replaced by a single election for all local government, on which public interest would be concentrated, this would give Labour a greater opportunity of exerting influence.

He was less than fair, however, in this dismissal of the opposition to the county councils. Firstly, there was not only the problem of travelling expenses. There was also the question of the time involved in travelling, which meant loss of earnings that working men could ill afford. Secondly, Struthers was writing as if the Commissioners of Supply, the forerunners of the county councils, were no longer in existence. True, the Local Government (Scotland) Act of 1889, which set up the county councils, deprived the Commissioners of Supply of most of their powers, but not all. From 1889 until 1929 they formed with the county councils joint committees to which all county council plans involving capital expenditure had to be submitted for approval [24]. Thus, by the proposals of the 1917 Bill, these landowners would have a certain say in such matters as the building of schools — a fact which gave Labour fears more substance than Struthers was willing to admit.

The opposition conducted by the school boards was a spirited one. In addition to the shoals of representations from individual boards, the Scottish School Boards Association produced a pamphlet giving the views of some well-chosen English educationists concerning the transfer of educational administration to the county councils [25]. One of the witnesses called was Michael Sadler, renowned for his work in comparative education conducted at the Office of Special Inquiries and

Reports, but by this time Vice-Chancellor of the University of Leeds. He was reported as having said in November 1916, that the complexity of educational administration had led to over-concentration of responsibility upon a few shoulders, to officialism and the strangling of initiative. There would, he was inclined to think, be a return in the future to *ad hoc* and to some form of proportional representation in the election of a local education authority. This testimony is less than satisfactory, predicting rather than prescribing a return to *ad hoc*, but the Association was able to produce for its next pamphlet a propaganda find of more value, with the report of an enquiry into the opinions of chief officers of education in England and Wales [26]. This investigation, conducted by E. H. Griffiths, Principal of University College, Cardiff, showed a majority of chief education officers in favour of *ad hoc* as in the days of the school boards.

Some doubt was thrown on the solidity of school board opposition to the bill by the allegation that the meeting of the Scottish School Boards Association at which the decision to attack the Bill was taken, was largely composed of ministers of the established church. The meeting was certainly held on a weekday, which was no doubt more convenient for ministers than others; and admittedly one of the main speakers was the Rev. John Smith, D.D., who launched a furious attack on what he called this 'retrograde, obscurantist and anti-democratic proposal', i.e. the mixing up of education 'with the management of drains and sewers, roads and bridges, tramways and electricity, water and gas' [27]. On the other hand, a number of individual school boards sent in their own protests, and we have no reason to think that the Church had any more say in these than was warranted by their representation on the boards.

The boards, it should be noted, were not opposed to change. They seem to have fully realized that at the very least there would have to be grouping of existing boards to provide viable administrative units. The Left unfortunately was not so clear on this question [28]. While the great majority of Labour organizations did see the need for larger areas, some are on record as opposing a reduction in the number of school boards, as 'detrimental to working-class representation'. Even if Struthers was right in thinking that Labour was poorly represented on the boards, there was undoubtedly an affection for them on the Left, and resentment at the Government's interference with what one I.L.P. branch significantly called 'the democratic control' of schools.

What was the attitude of teachers? As Struthers had noted, they had switched their allegiance from *ad hoc* and were ready to welcome the *ad omnia* county councils. Activists on teachers' associations can, it is true, be out of step with the bulk of membership, but such evidence as exists – for example, petitions from individual schools – points to a considerable measure of agreement on this throughout the profession. As early as 1916, the Scottish Education Reform Committee which represented the three main associations of teachers, the Educational Institute of Scotland, the Secondary Education Association of Scotland, and the Scottish Class Teachers' Federation, had decided in favour of the county councils as education authorities and had sent a deputation to the Secretary for Scotland in London on this and other aspects of their policy. It was their conversion which seems to have persuaded Struthers that an attack on *ad hoc* was worth a trial.

At the annual congress of the E.I.S. at the beginning of January 1918, their president, John Strong, attacked the Act of 1872 which had introduced the school boards. The principle of *ad hoc* could hardly be defended on the grounds of tradition, he pointed out, as education in Scotland had for 400 years been the concern of town councils, heritors (landowners) and presbyteries of the Church. None of these was *ad hoc*. Nor was the national parliament of the day.

This was a speech to gladden the heart of Sir John Struthers. He had in fact been shown it beforehand and had made some confidential observations on it [29]. The arguments against *ad hoc*, he believed, would have to be 'reiterated in season and out of season before the popular mind is cleared of certain strong prepossessions'.

The reason for his particular interest in this speech was that he thought the E.I.S. might have a crucial role to play. He had concluded that the fate of his Bill might depend on the attitude of the Labour Party and he knew that the E.I.S. was 'on cordial terms' with them. He hoped, therefore, that Strong would be able to use the E.I.S. to convert Labour to his way of thinking. He suggested that Strong should point to the spheres in which *ad hoc* could be seen at work, the public apathy concerning them, and the consequent lack of working class representation. He even thought that *ad omnia* county councils, which he trusted would attract more voters, would be a *more* democratic form of local administration. In his reply, the president of the E.I.S. thanked Struthers for this point about the Labour Party. It had been brought into his speech at Perth and the editor of *The Educational News* would be using it soon. 'We are making the most of [it],' he said [29].

Clearly the secretary of the Department was using every means at his disposal to see that this Bill, of which he had been the 'architect', was passed by parliament. On another occasion, having heard that J. M. Henderson, the MP for West Aberdeenshire, was about to oppose the abolition of the school boards, he wrote to a friend, R. H. N. Sellar asking him to use his influence with Henderson before the Scots Liberal MPs could be turned against the Bill [30].

Though the Government had the enthusiastic backing of the teachers, they had only lukewarm support from the bodies due to gain most from the Bill's proposals, namely the county councils. In March there were a few county councils which decided to support the Government on this issue, and in April the Association of County Councils finally consented to becoming the local authorities for education, but significantly added that 'a Bill of such importance should be delayed until the conclusion of peace'. This argument that important legislation should not be considered when so many men were still away at the front was, of course, normally heard only from the Bill's enemies.

By this time, however, support of any kind was almost certainly too late. The Government had already shown signs of weakening. Indeed, at least one observer had noticed the signs from the very beginning, for there is an unsigned note in the files of the Scotch Education Department remarking that Munro, even in introducing the Bill to the House of Commons, seemed to be saying 'we put forward county council management, but we shall change it, if you like' [31]. The first mention of a possible climb-down appeared in the newspapers in March. It appears that, at a private meeting on the 19th, the Scottish Liberal MPs had faced Munro with an ultimatum: the Government must keep the *ad hoc* principle or the Bill would be torpedoed. Munro in his turn had presented the Liberals with a choice. Either they agreed on an alternative, or he would withdraw the Bill completely. Munro knew, of course, that there was such a widespread realization of the need for change that there would be a considerable burden of unpopularity on those who were seen to obstruct the proposed legislation, particularly as a Bill dealing with education in England was clearly going to be passed that year [32].

Teachers were quick to sniff a change in government policy. The E.I.S. arranged a meeting with the Scottish Schools Boards Association in the hope of arranging a compromise between their opposing points of view. They even wrote to Munro inviting him to suggest 'very confidentially and privately' the lines along which such a settlement might be reached, but Munro declined to take any part in these negotiations. He did not, however, deny the report of his intentions which had caused the disputants to meet.

According to one report, the Secretary for Scotland had told the

Scottish Liberal MPs that, in order to save his Bill, he was prepared to concede the principle of *ad hoc*. The question then was, what would be the reaction of teachers to the Government's climb-down? They, after all, were not about to seek re-election; Munro *was*, and the extent of the magic which the 'coupon' was to wield could hardly be foreseen.

The feelings of the E.I.S. were soon made known to the Department. On 5 April their representatives met Struthers and said that they were prepared to consider *ad hoc* bodies provided the county area was retained. When they added that they understood that the Secretary for Scotland was prepared to go half-way to meet his critics in this way, Struthers, according to the official record of the interview, said that Munro had not told him this [33]. This seems extraordinary. It may be significant, however, that he did not deny all knowledge of what was going on. Indeed, no-one who had been reading the newspapers could have been genuinely surprised to hear of Munro's intentions. But there is a peevish note in the record of this interview and it seems that, at this point, relationships between the two men were somewhat strained. It is surely not too fanciful to see Munro's weakness, evident all along in his complete dependence on his chief civil servant, showing itself again in his failure to tell him openly that he had decided to abandon their position.

Struthers had to swallow his disappointment. After writing the draft of a speech for Munro to give to the T.U.C. at Ayr, a speech in which Munro stated publicly his willingness to compromise on the question of *ad hoc*, he got down to the details involved in retaining *ad hoc* education authorities with the county instead of the parish as the main unit of administration.

He produced a memorandum which included a number of practical suggestions [34]. The first showed Struthers' tenacity and his distrust of the *ad hoc* principle. This was a proposal to concede *ad hoc* in the case of the counties, but to introduce *ad omnia* in the cities. He had 'little doubt' but that the contrast between the two types of authority would lead to a rapid crumbling of the sentiment in favour of *ad hoc*. On the other hand, he suggested the Government could look again at the proposals he had drafted in 1913, which would have retained the boards, while making them in certain respects subordinate to joint committees of the school boards in each county [35].

The solution which Struthers found least unsatisfactory, however, was to disregard the parish and adopt a broader electoral division. A certain number of members of a new county authority could then be allotted to each division, and this in turn would permit the introduction of proportional representation. The advantage of this system of voting was that it would on the one hand ensure the representation of Roman Catholics without the need for co-option, and at the same time would avoid the undue influence given to minorities by the system of cumulative voting.

When the re-drafted Bill was introduced in Parliament in June, the reaction was generally favourable. 'Verily, Bottom, thou art translated,' exclaimed Sir Edward Parrott, but like most members, he approved of the change to *ad hoc* authorities. Perhaps, however, some of those who applauded the statesmanship shown by Munro in bowing to public pressure, did not listen carefully enough to the speech with which he introduced the second reading. He had, he said, made the change because of the opposition aroused by his original proposals, but he still believed that *ad omnia* authorities constituted the best solution from the educational point of view. More significantly, he added that he had made the change 'in view of the reform of local government — a reform which I believe to be imminent' [36]. As it happened, the reform of local government was delayed until 1929; but it seems worth noting that the Secretary for Scotland thought of *ad hoc* authorities as only a temporary expedient. If the whole of local government was soon to be in the melting-pot, it was no great concession that he was making.

The Bill received a second reading without a division. Of the fifteen speakers who made clear their attitude on the question of local authorities, only three were opposed to the new Bill. The other twelve, including nine of the ten Liberals and Barnes, the Labour member, spoke in support of *ad hoc*. The remaining stages of the Bill passed without incident and it received the royal assent on 21 November 1918.

Apart from the fact that the terms offered to the voluntary schools caused so little controversy — less, surely, than they would now — the striking feature of the passage of this Bill is the ease with which parliament accepted the new authorities, *ad hoc*, proportional representation and all. It was left to the member for Pontefract, Frederick Booth, to point out the anomaly in the administration of education in Britain. He complained of the government sending out Whips 'compelling this House to vote black one day and white another day'. He could see 'no earthly reason' why, if *ad hoc* was right for Glasgow, it should not be right for Manchester.

The doubts expressed concerning the Act were mainly on the Government side, but criticism of something as clearly popular as *ad hoc* educational administration, was perhaps muted by the thought of the impending election. Those of the Left who wanted no interference with the school boards were also silenced, but in another way; namely by the provision in the Act for the setting up of school management committees. Just as pro-school board sentiment in England had been mollified by the Balfour Act's Part III authorities, so the Munro Act of 1918 in Scotland achieved the same end by requiring education authorities to set up these local committees, designed to undertake the day-to-day running of an individual school or a small group of schools in a particular area. As Shaw, the Liberal member for Kilmarnock Burghs, put it, 'in many respects these committees will take the place of the school boards and many of us hope that the best of the personnel of the existing school boards will gravitate on to the school management committees.'

III

Were the education authorities, established after such controversy, a success? This is a very difficult question, not only because it leads us into the unanswerable question as to what different results would have followed the handing over of educational administration to the county councils, but because of the extremely trying circumstances in which the authorities had to work. The first elections were held in 1919, so that the new bodies were hardly established before there came the era of the 'Geddes Axe'. The cuts in educational expenditure demanded by the Government in both Scotland and England meant an impoverishment of the service and bitterness among the profession. The position throughout the rest of the 1920s was little better, so that the *ad hoc* authorities had little experience of working in an atmosphere of prosperity before they were abolished by the Local Government (Scotland) Act of 1929. It has consequently been argued, not only that these circumstances make fair assessment of the education authorities impossible, but that, if economic conditions had been more favourable, they might have lasted much longer. This I find hard to accept, as the main argument used to kill *ad hoc* control of education, the overlap with other services, could equally well have been used whatever the financial position had been. In any case, the public, though still willing to vote in considerable numbers, seems to have lost interest in the question of *ad hoc* versus *ad omnia*.

There was an early unfavourable verdict on the working of the Act. It came in 1920, after only a year of the establishment of the education authorities, when Munro was obliged to answer criticisms of the Act before an audience of Scottish MPs [37]. The criticisms came from the parish councils, who complained that rural areas were suffering on account of the method of levying the education rate. (This was raised from individual parishes in proportion to their share of the total valuation of the property in the county.) Rightly, the Secretary for Scotland refused to heed their premature judgement that the Act's scheme of administration was a failure. More noteworthy perhaps is the complaint by the parish councils of 'lavish expenditure' by the new authorities. Duties were being taken seriously, it seems, in the first flush of post-war enthusiasm and before the axe of Geddes fell.

Other verdicts came later. In 1924 the author of an unsigned Department memorandum on the working of the Act dealt with a number of minor difficulties which had arisen, for example the anomalies in rating, the woolliness of the Act on the duties of school management committees, etc. [38] The nearest to a general comment on the new authorities is that there was no reason to believe that the abolition of the school boards had led to a loss of local interest in education. Indeed, some difficulties had been caused by local pride in some places opposing the downgrading of a school, or the upgrading of a neighbouring school. On the whole, the writer seemed fairly pleased with the working of the Act, finding 'abundant evidence' that members of the education authorities 'took a broad view' of the requirements of the county as a whole.

Finally, when the education authorities had been given the *coup de grâce* by parliament, the annual report of the Committee of Council on Education in Scotland paid tribute to their work. There was reference to their 'zeal' 'in adverse conditions' and a general approval of their period of office as one which had been characterized by 'progress which is attested by definite evidence at practically every point'. This must be discounted however. The similarity to official pronouncements on the work of the school boards which had been delivered at the time of *their* demise, some of which were almost as congratulatory, shows that the Scotch Education Department was a pious observer of the principle of *de mortuis nil nisi bonum*.

There is one claim, however, that might be expected to be verifiable — that of local interest, which the advocates of *ad hoc* claimed as the great virtue of the system. (The teachers, though opposing *ad hoc*, probably started from the same premise — only what is 'local interest' to one is 'interference' to another.) The number who voted at the first election of education authorities in 1919 was barely 29 per cent, a figure which might conceivably have been higher if the voting system had been less complicated than that of the 'transferable vote'. At the triennial elections that followed in 1922, 1925 and 1928 the figure went up to 44 per cent, fell to 38 per cent and then rose again to 41 per cent. However, the Department, in the annual report for session 1927–8, pointed out that over the four elections there had been a continuous decline in the number of candidates. Also, the number of uncontested divisions was higher in 1928 than at any of the three previous elections. Local interest, therefore, did not seem very strong and there were even signs that it was fading. On the other hand, we must remember that the electorate can be divided into two groups, those with, and those without, children at school. The latter had much less incentive to vote, and the percentage of those most closely affected was presumably much higher than the figures for the adult population as a whole. This enables us to see these figures in perspective and makes them look more impressive in contrast to the voting for the county councils from 1929 onwards.

The comparison of voting figures for the *ad hoc* authorities and the *ad omnia* county councils, however, proves extremely complicated. In the first place, the newspapers give the percentage poll for only a few counties for the elections of 1929, 1932, and 1935. Secondly, there is the unknown weight to attach to the already mentioned non-involvement of the childless in the elections for the education authorities. Thirdly, the effect of the addition of women to the electoral register in 1918, is also an imponderable factor. What is known is that many women were initially loath to exercise their hard-earned right to vote. Fourthly, to be at all valid, the comparison of the two periods would have to take some account of the variations seen in the percentage polling at elections for parliament. Finally, where a number of seats are not contested, as happened in the elections for both the education authorities and the county councils, simple percentage polls are not enough to establish the level of public interest. The number of contests must also be considered.

If the case that the abolition of *ad hoc* led to a loss of local interest in educational affairs must remain 'not proven', there still remains the question of the drop in the number of candidates and of contested divisions at the elections during the *ad hoc* era, from 1919 to 1929. The simplest explanation of this is most likely to be correct. The important questions in education at this time were finance, and the development of post-primary education, both issues being decided at a national rather than a local level. Indeed the local authorities were not particularly relevant in these struggles. Not surprisingly, a recent study of the *ad hoc* authority for Dunbartonshire found that 'throughout the last years of the Authority's life, time and again one reads in the press that the monthly meeting was "very brief" or that there was "nothing of a contentious nature to report".' [39] It may seem remarkable that, in these circumstances, as many as 40 per cent of the electorate took the opportunity to vote, but the realities of power in educational matters may have been unknown to the public.

Whatever the reason, there was too little interest left in the working of the education authorities to provide any effective protest at their abolition. This came as a result of a Bill which was concerned with the whole of local government in Scotland and which was brought forward at the end of 1928 in the last months of Baldwin's government. There was some half-hearted opposition to the provision for education committees in the counties and major cities to act as education authorities, Labour being apprehensive about the powers of co-option being given to the councils, but the Government resisted successfully, and the Bill became law early the following year as the Local Government (Scotland) Act 1929. The difference between the opposition to the 1929 measure and the campaign against the Bill of 1917 was not simply one of degree, but of kind. In 1917–18 the opposition came from pressure-groups, political parties and interested individuals, but not Parliament. The campaign was well under way before the Commons had had any chance to debate the Bill properly. In 1929 there was, of course, opposition from the education authorities themselves: no-one likes to be abolished. But otherwise the attack was largely a parliamentary affair. There was far less popular backing for ad hoc.

In fact it seems there was nothing like the same interest amongst the general public about the way in which education was run, as there had been eleven years previously. Even the E.I.S., which decided to support the Bill, carried very little discussion of its implications in the columns of its official weekly publication, the *Scottish Educational Journal*. It may be that more people were convinced of the need to integrate the services of education, health and housing, or that fewer believed in the virtues of specially elected authorities for education. But there was an additional factor: perhaps because there had been too little time for the new authorities to win the same popular affection as the school boards had enjoyed, few Scots any longer saw the *ad hoc* administration of education as a burning issue.

Notes

References beginning ED are to the records of the Scotch or Scottish Education Department. These are lodged in the Scottish Record Office, Edinburgh.

[1] See J. Amery – *The Life of Joseph Chamberlain*, Vol.IV (London, 1951), Chap. XCVI. Chamberlain himself, it is true, had in December 1901, suggested the abolition of the boards, but again only as part of a package which included 'local option'. See Amery, p. 487.

[2] See E. Eaglesham – 'Planning the Education Bill of 1902', in *British Journal of Educational Studies*, IX, 1, November 1960.

[3] *The Educational News*, 19 April, 26 April and 21 June 1902 respectively.

[4] *The Scotsman*, 5 November 1902.

[5] See ED 14/13.

[6] *The Educational News*, 15 November 1902

[7] See the editorial in *The Educational News*, 9 May 1903.

[8] See *The Educational News*, 17 January 1903.

[9] *The Educational News*, 31 January 1903. The vagueness of Lord Balfour's expression may well have been deliberate. The decision in favour of *ad hoc*, it seems, was not taken until later that year. See the correspondence dated (in pencil) July 1903, in ED 14/13.

[10] See 'Teachers and Security of Tenure, 1872–1908' in T. R. Bone (ed.), *Studies in the History of Scottish Education, 1872–1939*, London, 1967.

[11] James Mackintosh, 'Scottish Educational Reform', in *Scottish Liberal Association – Current Politics from a Liberal Standpoint*, London, 1905.

[12] Approval of the Bill was not universal (see W. M. Haddow, *My Seventy Years*, Chap.10, Glasgow, 1943), but there was no division over the second reading in parliament.

[13] Article reprinted in Robert Munro, Lord Alness, *Looking Back: fugitive writings and sayings*, London, 1930. Original source not given.

[14] Quoted by A. Morgan, *Makers of Scottish Education*, London, 1929.

[15] ED 14/142.

[16] See W. Ferguson, *Scotland, 1689 to the Present*, pp.374–9, Edinburgh, 1968.

[17] Memorandum of 9 May 1917 in ED 14/155.

[18] A. J. Belford, *Centenary Handbook of the Educational Institute of Scotland*, p.150, Edinburgh, 1946.

[19] H. A. L. Fisher, *An Unfinished Autobiography*, p. 106, London, 1940.

[20] For a full account of this aspect of the Bill see Rev. Brother Kenneth, F.M.S., 'The Education (Scotland) Act, 1918, in the Making,' in *The Innes Review*, XIX, 2, Autumn, 1968.

[21] Memoranda of 29 December 1917 (in ED 14/142) and 17 January 1918 (in ED 14/159).

[22] J. G. Kellas, 'The Mid-Lanark By-election (1888) & the Scottish Labour Party (1888–1894),' in *Parliamentary Affairs*, Vol. XVIII. 3, 1964–65.

[23] The 5th Schedule, section 5(b) of the Education (Scotland) Act, 1918, did allow education authorities to pay members for both travel and loss of earnings incurred in attending meetings, but county councillors continued to pay their own expenses until the passing of the Local Government (Scotland) Act, 1929.

[24] See G. S. Pryde, *Central and Local Government in Scotland since 1707*, London, 1960.

[25] See ED 14/84/2266.

[26] ED 14/86/2435, pamphlet entitled 'Education (Scotland) Bill, 1917 – Report of the Commission on the Council System of Educational Administration in England', London, 1918.

[27] See ED 14/82/2113.

[28] See especially ED/14/82.

[29] ED 14/136 cf. ED 14/83/2147.

[30] Letter of 26 January 1918 – see ED 14/82/2093a.

[31] ED 14/82/2076.

[32] See *Glasgow Herald*, 20 March 1918 and ED 14/85/2343, 2344.

[33] ED 14/104.

[34] Memorandum of 9 May 1918 in ED 14/157.

[35] Memorandum of 30 October 1913, in ED 14/159. The date of this document has been changed in pencil to 1917, but the reference of 9 May 1918, shows this to be incorrect.

[36] Hansard, 5th series, CVII, col. 1076.

[37] Address of 10 November 1920, in ED 14/141.

[38] See ED 14/160. For the effects of this woolliness, see A. F. B. Roberts, 'The Operation of the *Ad Hoc* Education Authority in Dunbartonshire between 1919 and 1930', in T. R. Bone (ed.), *Studies in the History of Scottish Education, 1872–1939*, London, 1967.

[39] A. F. B. Roberts, op. cit., p. 276.

Index